MW00711425

THE VALLEYS OF LIFE

Thank you! Everything in me says "thank you"!

THE MOMENT I *called* OUT,
YOU *stepped* IN; *you* MADE MY LIFE LARGE
with strength! psalms 138:4,4
THE MESSAGE

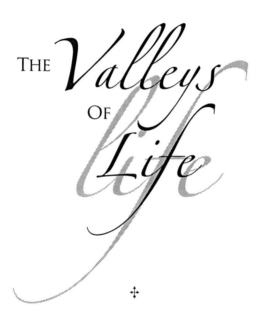

THE Valleys OF Life

JEFFREY E. MCLOUD

The Valleys of Life Published by Jeffrey E. McLoud

Website fortammyssake.com

Email jeff@investmentsholding.com

© Jeffrey E. McLoud 2005

Scripture quotations are taken from the *Holy Bible, New International Version*. NIV. Copyright © 1973, 1978, 1984 by International Bible Society. *The Message*. Copyright © 1993, 1994, 1985 by Eugene H. Peterson. *New Living Translation*. Copyright © 1997 Tyndale House Publishers, Inc. *New King James Version*. Copyright © 1979, 1980, 1982 by Thomas Nelson, Inc.

All rights reserved. No part of this publication may be reproduced, stored in a retrieval system, or transmitted in any form or by any means—electronic, mechanical, photocopying, recording, or otherwise—without the prior written permission of the publisher and copyright owners.

Design by Jakki Parker

Typeset in Gill Sans Light 10pt

Printed by Lightning Source Inc.

ISBN 0-9776484-2-7

DEDICATION

TO MY WIFE, TAMMY
The bravest most courageous person I have ever known.

TO CORY & KATELYNN
Your trust in Jesus has never wavered.

TO YOU
I surrender my life to always be husband and father.

ACKNOWLEGEMENTS

There are so many who have joined us in prayer, brought meals, stayed through the night at the hospital, sent cards, etc. We are eternally grateful to each of you! I just want to express my thanks to the body of Christ for blessing us in so many ways!

Mom and Dad — thanks for being the parents every child wishes they had. I love you! Bev — Do you remember our quiet times of worship in the hospital? What a blessing. Do you remember the simpler days when we thought life couldn't be any grander than staying up late on Friday night and watching Dean Martin and Jerry Lewis movies? What dorks we were/are! I love you! Amber — thanks for holding my hand while the mean nurse tried to torture me! Aunt Barbara and family — thanks for your daily visits, for praying with me, and trying to help us understand "medical jargon". We love you! Aunt Joanie and family — your visits were always like a ray of sunshine. The peace and presence of the Lord is with you wherever you go.

Thanks, Carolyn, for doing my laundry. Thanks, Betty, for doing the housework. Thanks Daniel for the beautiful website and thanks Dani for organizing meals. What a blessing to my family! To my MITI prayer group — you are my sisters at heart! Willie and Lois — We love you guys! Thanks for the sign idea. Too bad the devil, I mean the city, had to take them down! Lois, thanks for being my personal nurse and cheerleader. Mystie and Kody — You guys are special. Thanks for organizing meals, your prayers and love. Who would volunteer to stay with me the night I came off Morphine? A true friend! I will never forget waking up throughout the night and seeing you at the foot of my bed praying for me. Joni — thanks for taking me to treatment and for being my buddy.

Thanks, Kelly and Marci for supporting your brother. Gene, Jack and Donna thanks for being Jeff's parents and quietly loving him. Thank you, Kriers and Peltons for your love and support! We love you! Thanks, John and Richo, for being Jeff's mates. Terry and Shelly — thanks for being the neighbors we always wanted and never had! Thank you, Sonic & IHI family. Pastor Ted and Ginny — thank you for your wisdom and encouragement. Thanks to Pastors Mark & Tami, Mickey & Glenda, Roger & Elaine, Mark Guinn, Cousin Brian & Cousin David, Shon and Dwight for your prayers and support. To Daniel and Shirley thank you for helping us see our future to help others overcome their battles.

To our foreign friends: Bobby & Noemi, Monroe, Pastora Navarro, Pastor Domeng and Fely and all the Filipino pastors and churches — thank you for standing in faith with us. Mario and Celeste — greetings in South Africa. We enjoy your visits and are blessed to call you our friends. Jaime in Columbia — thanks for your prayers. We bless you in Jesus' name. Brother Mitchell and Odena in Samoa — thank you for joining us in prayer from the other side of the world! Global Advance and the Shibleys — we love you all! Thank you for touching the world for Jesus! To our Brazilian buddies — Cello, Claudia, and Bruna, we love you. Thank you for your love and prayers. So glad the US is finally willing to let you call this home!

To all the Doctors: Shetty, Hanson, Wolfe — thanks for your determination to help us win. To Dr. Toma: thanks for giving extra time in answering all our questions and keeping focused on our goal. The P.A., nurses, caregivers — you made a miserable experience a little easier to tolerate; thank you very much.

To Cory and Katelynn — You bless me more than you can imagine. I am so proud of you both! You have stood toe to toe with a giant and never flinched. Your faith and courage challenges me! I LOVE YOU!!!

To Jeff: You have been a pillar of strength for me! I am so thankful that you are my partner in life. You are my soul mate, my best, good friend — and still my inspiration! LOVE YOU!!!!!

Thank you, Jesus, for walking with us on this journey. You deserve all honor and glory for the miracle you are working in our lives! *Tammy* xx

CONTENTS

Chapter 1   The Valleys of Life 19

Chapter 2   10 Biblical Truths 25

Chapter 3   The Positive in the Negative 31

Chapter 4   Life in Christ 37

Chapter 5   Praise and Humility 43

Chapter 6   God's Benefits 49

Chapter 7   The Battle for Life 55

Chapter 8   Appointed to Triumph 61

Chapter 9   Troubles Without Being Troubled 67

Chapter 10   The Lord is, He Will 73

Chapter 11   Prayer; More Than Asking to Receive 79

Chapter 12   A Real Life Partner 85

Chapter 13   Cause and Effect 91

Chapter 14   God the Caregiver 97

Chapter 15   God Your Friend 103

CONTENTS

Chapter 16	The Lord Your Guardian	109
Chapter 17	Life's Choices	115
Chapter 18	What are you thinking?	121
Chapter 19	The Blood of Christ	127
Chapter 20	Redeemed for Life	133
Chapter 21	You ARE a Winner!	139
Chapter 22	God's Declaration of Righteousness	145
Chapter 23	No Quid Pro Quo	151
Chapter 24	Intimacy with Jesus	157
Chapter 25	The Security of Our Father	163
Chapter 26	You, Your, You Are	169
Chapter 27	Destined to Die, so We Could Live	175
Chapter 28	Faithful God	181
Chapter 29	The Lord our Righteousness	187
Chapter 30	Insight for our Daily Living	193
Chapter 31	Wisdom from Heaven	199

INTRODUCTION

March 4th 2005 is a day that our family was forever changed. I received a phone call from Dr. Mark Mellow that a cancerous tumor was located in the duodenum of my wife Tammy's small bowel. Within 3 hours she was on her way to surgery. What the doctors thought would be a quick and relatively simple procedure turned out to be anything but.

Upon opening her up they discovered that the cancer had spread to her ovaries and uterus and was all over her pelvic wall. After consulting with the University of Oklahoma the decision was made to do a full hysterectomy. 4-1/2 hours of surgery later and subsequent pathology reports confirmed a diagnosis of "Stage 4, small bowel carcinoma". About 2 weeks later it was discovered that the small bowel cancer had also formed a tumor in her liver. The doctors decided that surgery at this time should be postponed until they are convinced subsequent treatments are shrinking it.

The doctors have said that "small bowel" cancer occurs in only 1-1.4 percent out of every 100,000 cases, or about 2000 - 5000 cases per year compared to 150,000 cases of colon cancer annually. Consequently, little is know about his type of cancer and its successful treatment. Survival statistics are only 30 percent of people live longer than 2 years. We have informed the doctors that we are not interested in the extension of life, rather a complete cure. They have said that "they have seen miracles" and "if she is cured you will not be thanking any doctors". None the less, they have agreed to help us pursue our goal of total recovery in "facilitating a miracle, not performing one", as one doctor said.

Prior to March 4th Tammy had spent an additional 6 weeks in the hospital since about the first of the year. She could not keep food down, and she was being treated for an entirely different problem from the cancer.

The next 2 weeks of post-op, Tammy remained in the hospital recovering from surgery. The shock and trauma on our family was just that, shock! That is when family, friends, and church members literally from all around the world began to mobilize for us in prayer.

But let me take you back to August of 2004. I was in prayer one morning when I heard the whisper, and I mean whisper of God's Spirit in my heart say… "Why don't you consider investing more of your time, talent, and treasure into your family". It was so quiet, so gentle, so off the subject, I still to this day do not know how I heard it.

I was far from a bad husband and father, but my career in the family business and missions ministry consumed most of my passion not to mention my time, talent, and treasure. I struggled with this "Word" because as I thought it through and prayed about it, it seemed God wanted me to resign from all my missions' commitments. To even resign them mentally, as if to say, "You are done here, so do not even think about it anymore".

It seemed that the Lord wanted me to quit giving my "offering" money to His "Great Commission" and re-invest it into my kids, my wife, and our home. I was heart broken and really battled whether this was even scriptural. The longer I waited to act, the more turmoil I was creating in my soul.

So on October 4th, 2004 I drafted and sent a letter to all my missions contacts telling them of my plan. I cannot tell you how many gallons of tears I shed over the next few weeks. Then again at the same time a renewed love and passion for my family came that I had not experienced in almost 20 years of marriage.

So I began investing time, talent, and treasure into my family. I remember talking to my good friend and Great Commission partner David Shibley about my decision. He was reminded of a great military strategist's words when he said, "Always advance from a secure position". That was it! Now I understood! He explained to me that as we move forward in this fight to advance God's Kingdom, I needed to do so with complete security within my own base.

Sometime in February after Tammy had come home from her first 3 week stay in the hospital, I woke up early in the morning. Before I could register a thought and just before my eyes actually opened I heard these words in my heart as loud as a jet engine, "I have a message from Jesus and He says that when you walk through the valley of the shadow of death do not be afraid for He is with you". It knocked the air out of me. I had no idea what that could mean, and I never even thought until months later that is was applicable to Tammy's subsequent surgery and future treatment.

I never told anyone except my family about this until after the surgery. I am so grateful to Jesus for His Words. Not only has that Word sustained our family through this whole ordeal, but the encouragement and love we received was overwhelming. We never realized just how many people really loved us.

As people came to the hospital to visit, we asked them to write a note of encouragement to Tammy or a scripture verse. Soon cards, letters, and emails from around the globe came not only for Tammy, but our entire family as well. Needless to say, but sometimes that card, note, or scripture would be like a special delivery letter sent directly to us from heaven itself for that moment in time. This happened several times a day as we would try and absorb the magnitude of what had just happened.

I was so impressed by this and we respected EVERYONE'S word of scripture. Another friend of mine, Pastor Ted Estes who happens to be cancer free from a fight several years ago, began to encourage us to begin confessing the Word of God daily. It was one of the things he did to arrive at his complete, medically confirmed healing. So I had the thought, "Why not take the scriptures everyone had sent us and begin to do that?" So we did.

I had another idea to group several like-themed verses together. I studied them, researched Greek and Hebrew words, and used synonyms to expound and give greater depth and insight. I then took all those ingredients and formed them into a recipe for our personal paraphrase. The "My Confession" pages you will read in this book are that very thing.

It took several weeks to write them all out, but every evening for several months, Tammy and I, Cory and Katelynn would read these aloud together. A special treat would always be when family members or friends would drop by and read them with us.

As time went by and we did this, our family became full of faith; firm and resolved in the fact that not only will Tammy be completely healed and restored to normal health, but we could encourage others that are going through similar trials in life.

Then another idea came; why not take each confession, give my personal thoughts and insights on it, outline it and write it so it could be a devotional book. I have never written a book before, but I have harbored a secret ambition to do so.

If only I had stayed awake through English class all those years. After all, "Writing is stupid"; was my logic back then.

The real motivation to write this book was honestly to give back something to all the people that sent cards, left scripture, and sent emails. I do not know how we could have made it through what we did without those people. So family and friends, this book is for you. This is the best way we know how to say thank you. Let it in turn bless you the way it has ministered to us.

You can always check on Tammy's medical update by clicking onto

www.fortammyssake.com

Click to the link on the homepage and then medical updates.

Reveal yourself to me Lord!

THE *Valleys* OF *Life*

CHAPTER ONE

Those WHO LIVE IN THE SHELTER OF

THE MOST *high* WILL FIND REST IN THE

SHADOW OF THE *almighty*. HE ALONE

IS MY *refuge*, MY PLACE OF SAFETY; HE

IS MY GOD AND I AM *trusting* HIM.

Psalm 91:1-2 (NLT)

My Confession

I will obey the message of Jesus that when I walk, proceed, and move forward into my future through this valley I am experiencing, the shadow of death, its darkness, and distress, WILL NOT cause me to be afraid. The unpleasant and miserable things have no effect on my mind or the faith of my future because you, Jesus, are personally walking through this valley with me. I continue to dwell in the secret place of the Most High God. I am abiding under HIS shadow. I say of the Lord, "You are my refuge and my fortress; My God, in you will I trust."

✛

PSALMS 23:4 · PSALM 91:1, 2

THE *V*ALLEYS OF *L*IFE

A valley generally consists of a lower elevation than the peaks that surround it. The peaks of life seem to be the pleasant moments when everything goes our way or according to our plans. The valleys are widely thought to be times in our life when circumstances are bad and unpleasant. The "valleys" are things no human is exempt from. Someone once said "stuff happens". But why? Why us? Why now? A million people would have a million answers to why, but even if you knew "why" what good does that do you now? Bad things just happen to good people. Your unpleasant circumstances do not change the way God sees you, though. His first action toward you is always love, mercy, and grace — NOT judgment the way some think. The real question is not why, but how; how do I make it through this?

Five Suggestions:

1. Keep walking. Do not quit. Maintain hope. As long as you do not quit, every day of progression is another day closer to your deliverance from your trouble.

2. Do not be afraid. Fear is the opposite of faith. Fear will cause you to doubt and not believe the truth of God's word.

3. Build up your faith by hearing and confessing with your mouth the truth of the word of God concerning your situation. Remember, there are always facts about your circumstance, but they may not be the truth of what God has said.

4. Know you are not alone. God promises to be with you. Some of the greatest encounters of grace you will ever experience come in times of crisis.

5. Take time to get alone with God. The secret place is that intimate place where you fellowship and commune with God alone.

You really only have two choices; you can stay under the *shadow of your circumstance* or take refuge under the *shadow of God.* Walk through and keep moving through the unpleasant circumstance, but do not give in. Continually stay and come into the fortress of God's shadow, his presence, the place of hope. What you will discover is not the "why" of my circumstances; not the "when" will this end; rather the "who". You will discover a loving, caring, merciful, and gracious God in a way you could NEVER have imagined before. Remember it is God Himself who promised He would walk through it with you. If you let Him, He will guide you back to the mountain top.

✛

PRAYER: Ask for God to reveal Himself to you.
MEMORIZE & MEDITATE: Psalms 91:1, 2
FAITH ACTION: Speak only God's truth.

Life is not ruined, just changing!

10 Biblical Truths

CHAPTER TWO

THE *Spirit* OF GOD, WHO RAISED JESUS

FROM THE DEAD, *lives* IN YOU. AND JUST

AS HE RAISED CHRIST FROM DEAD, HE WILL

GIVE *life* TO YOUR MORTAL BODY BY THE

SAME SPIRIT LIVING WITHIN *you*.

Romans 8:11 (NLT)

My Confession

The Spirit of Almighty God who raised Jesus from the dead is living in me, so that just as he truly raised Christ from the dead he will also give life to my earthly and human body through his Spirit, who lives in me. You are the treasure in my body and the excellence of your power is not of me. I am not crushed; I am not in despair; I am not forsaken; I am not destroyed; but I desire to always carry about in the body the dying of the Lord Jesus, that the life of Jesus also may be manifested in my body.

✛

ROMANS 8:11 · II CORINTHIANS 4:7-10

10 BIBLICAL TRUTHS

1. God raised Jesus from the dead.

2. That same Spirit now lives in you.

3. That Spirit gives life to your human body.

4. That Spirit in you is a valuable, endless treasure.

5. Success rests not in your ability, but in God's authority.

6. Bad circumstances do not regulate the good in your future.

7. Your situation is not hopeless.

8. God has not forgotten about you.

9. Life is not ruined, just changing.

10. God wants to use you to reveal Himself to others.

The most fundamental doctrine of the Christian faith is that Jesus Christ was crucified and raised from the dead. This belief is what qualifies us to be "born again" and receive eternal life. If you have believed in this truth, then you need to understand everything else God has done for you. Eternal life is not heaven. It is the perpetual style of living that exhibits the attributes of God, both now AND in heaven. God's main purpose is to populate heaven and His life in you allows you to bring others to Christ. It is His life in us that allows us to really experience the life He intended for man, and we are examples to the rest of the world.

When you accepted Christ as your Savior it was not just your spirit that was made alive; HIS Spirit was placed in your body. Adam received the "breath" of life from God while he was dirt, and he became a "living being". Jesus "breathed" on the disciples and said, "Receive the Holy Spirit". You have God's Spirit inside to exhibit to everyone around you that Jesus is alive and exists. Together with other believers we make up the "body of Christ" or the complete manifestation of the living God on the earth — His attributes, His character, His actions, His life.

Life is always evolving, growing, and changing — look at nature as an example. Your life is no different; just because you cannot see something now does not mean it does not exist. Just look at an apple seed. Can you see apples? Can you see a tree? No, of course not, but inside it has the ability to make apples. What does it lack to do so? Time, the proper environment, and the right ingredients. Very simply, that is what God is doing in your life by his Spirit that is living in you. God is continually working in you to change your attributes, your character, your actions, your life. Remember, God is working to change and improve your life for the better, so you can experience the abundant life He has provided. Remember though, that God is as interested in saving others as He was in saving you. Others MUST see Jesus in you as well.

✢

PRAYER: Thank God for his Spirit in you.

MEMORIZE & MEDITATE: Romans 8:11

FAITH ACTION: Obey the Spirit inside you every moment.

For you will cause me to flourish!

The Positive
In The
Negative

I *know* WHAT I AM DOING. I HAVE IT

ALL PLANNED OUT — *plans* TO TAKE CARE

OF YOU, NOT ABANDON YOU, PLANS TO *give*

YOU THE *future* YOU HOPE FOR.

Jeremiah 29:11 (The Message)

My Confession

I know I have victory and will triumph in this difficulty and hardship, because the hardship will produce perseverance, resolve and determination to never ever quit or give into this difficulty I face every day. As a result or consequence, Godly character is developing in me, and that forces me to look forward to and anticipate the accomplishments of the purposes and dreams God has set forth in my heart to do. I am not disappointed in blind optimism, because the love of God has been poured out in my heart by the Holy Spirit who was given to me. I know that God has thoughts and plans for my future; thoughts of peace, prosperity, health and tranquility. God's plans are to use my body to reveal the riches of glory to all that are currently lost without him.

✠

ROMANS 5:3-5 · JEREMIAH 29:11 · COLOSSIANS 1:27

THE *POSITIVE* IN THE *NEGATIVE*

Only an all-powerful God could take a hardship in life and turn it into a training time to further His purposes in us. God is much more interested in what you become than what you accomplish. If He can develop Godly character in you, then you become qualified to fulfill His plans for your life. Just look at the life of Jesus — 30 years training as a son, carpenter and businessman, for 3 years of ministry. He lived His life in obscurity 90.9 percent and only 9.1 percent of His life fulfilling his ultimate call. The training and shaping in your life by the Holy Spirit is the most important thing you can do today. It prepares you for your future. God can accomplish in a few years in our life what would take us a lifetime to achieve on our own without Him.

God's recipe for Success

- Learn to rejoice and be grateful for God's faithfulness in the past during your current difficulty.

- Know that your hardship puts you in position not to quit or give in.

- By not giving in, you begin to change and develop the Godly character the Father intends for your life.

- With the Godly character maturing in you, the expectations of good things progress in your life.

- You now are competent to understand the goodness and the love of God for you that God has placed in you by the Holy Spirit.

What is the blueprint or plan God has for your future? Only He knows, but its ingredients include, peace, prosperity (family, health, financial), tranquility and serenity. Is this not what every person on earth wants and pursues? People spend a whole life in pursuit of these things, and some never find them. God wants you to have them all. The world pursues "things and stuff" thinking they are the keys to life, rather than the giver of life, Jesus Christ Himself. We find this abundant life Jesus spoke of in an interpersonal relationship with Him. You cannot do it your way and still find it. It is Christ's Holy Spirit that is in control of your life. He is the one who teaches us, leads us, guides us, and reminds us of all things. When you are surrendered to Him and His purpose, He brings us into that abundant life. Even when life seems negative, we should remember God is always bringing us to the positive. He is after all the author, the architect, and builder of life. If your life has more negatives than positives, try the above "life's recipes for success".

✢

PRAYER: Thank God for your future.

MEMORIZE & MEDITATE: Jeremiah 29:11, 12

FAITH ACTION: Submit yourself to change.

I surrender my all to you my God!

Life In Christ

I MYSELF NO LONGER LIVE BUT *Christ* LIVES

IN ME. SO I LIVE MY **LIFE** IN THIS EARTHLY BODY BY

trusting IN THE SON OF GOD, WHO

LOVED ME AND GAVE **HIMSELF** FOR *me*.

Galatians 2:20 (NLT)

My Confession

I have in the past, and continue through the present, and into my future committed my life to your purposes. I am crucified with Christ, and it is no longer I that live, but Christ that lives in me; and the life which I now live in the body, I live through faith in the Son of God who loved me and gave Himself up to death on my behalf. I consider my life not my own but under the Lordship of the King of kings, Jesus Christ who purchased me with His own blood. Therefore, I will glorify Christ in my body which is God's property and not my own.

✛

GALATIANS 2:20 · 1 CORINTHIANS 6:19, 20

LIFE IN CHRIST

Life in Christ is NOT what most people imagine it is. Living a life in Christ is a lifestyle of trust in His Spirit and obedience to His Word daily and moment by moment. As humans we tend to want to know the "why" before we act. We want to know the path and direction of the journey before we move. We must understand things, it must make sense. We feel pressure around us to be perfect in all our actions. So instead of moving, we stand still because we are unwilling to take a chance. Fear of failure, fear of being ridiculed causes us to stand still. This is not the lifestyle of faith. This is not the life in Christ. If faith is truly the substance or tangible evidence of what we are hoping for, then faith not put into action leads to hopelessness and depression. In order to move into the abundant life of Christ, we must understand the following:

- You must be devoted to Christ and entrust your life into His hands.

- When you trust Him, He will live through you.

- God loves you unconditionally, and your acceptance by Him is not dependent on your behavior.

- Jesus surrendered and sacrificed His life so you could live the life He has predetermined for you.

- Since He purchased you and you trust Him with your eternal soul, you must surrender to the authority of His Spirit and His Word.

- Your purpose in life is for His glory.

⊛　Your will and your life are no longer under your ownership.

Considering these seven things, you can see that to do them requires supreme trust. Does God really love me? Will God really do what is best for my future? Is he going to force me to do things I do not want to do? Here is a better question... if you could always be living your life in hindsight, would your life be better off than it is? If you could go back and rewrite your own personal history, would your present circumstance be the same? You can live that way! God is present and already in your future. He sees you not as you are, but what you will be. Every step, every change He has you make is always with the goal of an improved, abundant life in mind. What would the world be like if we could accurately predict the future? Better yet what would the world be like if people entrusted their lives to a God who already lives in the future? This is trust, this is faith. If you can look beyond where you are now with a hope that God has a far greater future for you, then you can have real life in Christ.

✢

PRAYER: Recommit yourself to God's purposes.

MEMORIZE & MEDITATE: Galatians 2:20

FAITH ACTION: Yield to the Holy Spirit to change.

My soul longs, for you are all I need!

Praise AND Humility

But *he* was wounded and crushed for

our sins. He was *beaten* that we

MIGHT have peace. He was whipped.

and we were *healed!*

Isaiah 53:5 (NLT)

My Confession

I choose today to praise you, Lord, for you have saved me from my enemies. You refuse to let them triumph over me. O Lord my God, I pleaded with you, and you gave me my health again. You brought me back from the brink of the grave, from death itself, and here I am alive. You came to earth and died for me; now I have abundant life. By your stripes I am healed, for nothing is impossible with you. You show your might and strength in my presence, and I am strong in you and in your power, love and the sound mind you have given to me. God truly is my shepherd and I shall lack no good thing. God is my helper, so I will not be afraid.

✛

PSALMS 30: 1-3 · JOHN 10:10 · ISAIAH 53:5

LUKE 1:37 · ZEPHANIAH 3:17

PRAISE AND HUMILTY

You cannot earn God's favor. There is nothing that you can do to make Him prove His love for you. God simply wants to be believed. However, when you understand how needy you are and helpless you are without God and humble yourselves before Him, you are no longer an enemy He opposes but a candidate for His favor. Praising and thanking God with your mouth releases an attitude that counteracts pride. It is the acknowledgement that God has done something you are incapable of doing by yourself. A lack of praise in your life is silent admission of self-sufficiency. The real problem then is all you will ever do in life is all you can do on our own. When you live a life of praise and thanksgiving for what God has done (past), what He is doing (present), He will reveal Himself in your future. Praise is a decision, a choice – not an emotion. It is an admission that you recognize God in your life. Take note of all that God will do on your behalf:

- Saves you from your enemy.
- Enemies will not triumph over you.
- Restores your health.
- Delivers you from death.
- Gives you life.
- Provides you abundant life.
- Heals your sickness.
- Does the impossible for you.
- Exhibits His power to you.

- Makes you strong in His power

- Causes you to love.

- Gives you a mind capable of making good decisions.

- Becomes your continual guide for future direction.

- You will lack nothing.

- Helps when you cannot do it alone.

- Gives you courage.

Are you capable of doing these things on your own? God extends grace or His unearned favor and blessing when we humble ourselves and admit we need Him. If by your actions you eliminate God's influence in your life, then you become God's enemy. But even then God will not destroy you; no, you will destroy yourself. If life has become messy and out of control because of your unwillingness to follow God's ways and His Word, then simply change your mind, go the other way and follow after Him. Then begin to give God thanks and praise for what He will do in your future. If He has helped you in the past do you think He will neglect you in the future? Of course not, so make the decision to pursue Jesus.

✢

PRAYER: Praise God for your future.

MEMORIZE & MEDITATE: John 10:10

FAITH ACTION: Stop complaining, and start praising.

O my soul, forget not all His benefits!

God's Benefits

CHAPTER SIX

PRAISE THE *Lord*, I TELL MYSELF, AND NEVER

FORGET THE GOOD *things* HE DOES FOR ME!

Psalms 103:2 (NLT)

My Confession

I bless the Lord by making a willful decision that everything inside me with all my energy and strength will pay tribute to my Lord and Master; acclaim and honor the Lord, O my soul, and forget not all His benefits: He forgives all my iniquities by His mercy, and heals all my diseases by His grace; He redeemed my life from destruction, ruin, and extermination. It is God Himself who said He is the God that heals sickness and disease. He crowns me with loving-kindness and tender mercies; He satisfies my mouth with good things, so that my youth is renewed like the eagles.

✢

PSALM 103:1-5 · EXODUS 15:26

GOD'S BENEFITS

When considering employment and the wages given, it is also important to take into account the "benefits". These consist of things like paid vacations, health insurance, retirement plans, and company cars, etc. A benefit is an advantage, help, or assistance. Most employers do not place a cash value on these things. In other words they are a part of the total salary package. If you choose not to use them they cannot be redeemed in the form of more money. You use it, or you lose it.

God has given us benefits also. We all have them and they are available to us, but some use them while others do not. Believe they are available, receive them, and act on them by faith is all we do to activate them. Don't be a faithless Christian that believes que sera sera, whatever will be will be. "If God wants me to have these things, He will give them to me." Let your faith rise to the standard of God's Word; never bring God's Word down to your current circumstances and call that "God's will". Let's see what some of God's benefits are.

1. He pardons all your current sin and character faults.
2. He cures physical sickness and disease.
3. Like a wealthy relative He purchased your life so that you would have an abundant life and never die.
4. He protects you from attacks with His favor and good deeds toward you.
5. He makes sure that we are full and have enough of His bountiful goodwill so that others can see and acknowledge it.
6. He energizes your life with vision and hope so that you feel young again.

He pardons, cures, purchases, protects, fills, and energizes. Anything here you need that you did not know was yours? 2 Peter 1:3 says, *"His divine power has given us everything we need for life and godliness through our knowledge of him…"* God has provided for your well-being on earth everything you need to achieve what He wants you to accomplish. You can never know you have these things without *"knowledge of him"*. Without an intimate relationship with Christ's Holy Spirit these "benefits" seem far away, impossible, or for someone else. Here is the secret… the benefits are not what you need to seek and pursue; pursue relationship with the living Christ, get to know him personally, and when you do faith and confidence to receive His benefits will just happen. Would any person today refuse everything they need for life from an employer? Know what your benefits are by knowing God.

✢

PRAYER: Match your needs to God's benefits and tell Him.

MEMORIZE & MEDITATE: Psalms 103:3-5

FAITH ACTION: Talk about and confess God's benefits, not your lack.

For my confidence rests in You!

THE *Battle* FOR *Life*

CHAPTER SEVEN

THE LORD IS MY *light* AND SALVATION —

SO WHY SHOULD I BE AFRAID? THE LORD

protects ME FROM DANGER —

SO WHY SHOULD I *tremble?*

Psalms 27:1 (NLT)

My Confession

The Lord is my healing light and my source of deliverance from all sickness and disease; I will not be afraid of my current situation because the Lord is the strength of my life; of whom shall I be afraid? The Lord has a stranglehold on my life – why would I be scared and anxious in this circumstance? Though my enemy surrounds and attempts to overwhelm me, my heart will not fear: though war and fighting for my life break out against me, even then I will be confident.

✛

PSALMS 27:1

THE *B*ATTLE FOR *L*IFE

Our family is very keen and aware of this subject. At the time of this writing my wife is in a battle of life and death with a rare form of cancer. The fact is only 30 percent of people with this type live beyond 2 years. Even though she is receiving state of the art medical treatment, our hope is in God and His promises. Daily the medical facts are before us, yet God's truth supersedes medical fact. We believe, confess, and hold firmly to these truths and principles.

Truths and Principles

- God is the source of healing. He uses others as His instruments.
- We will not be afraid. It is a choice.
- The Lord is our strength. We rely on Him.
- We realize He has a firm grip on us. He desires life, too.
- We are not afraid of medical facts.
- We do not get in a hurry about medical decisions.
- We understand that an enemy wants to kill my wife.
- Still we choose not to be afraid.
- We are in a battle, and we will fight back. We choose to resist.
- Our confidence in God is greater than at any point in our life.

One common theme that runs through this verse is fear. I have said it once, I will say it again — fear is a choice, a decision of your will. Fear is the result of unbelief; unbelief has only one cure — repentance. In order for man to receive anything from

God, forgiveness, answer to prayer, etc. it requires faith. *"Without faith it is impossible to please God"* Hebrews 11:6. Therefore unbelief is the one thing that ties the hand of God to move. Promises are available to all; receiving and implementing them is only for those who choose to believe.

Listen friend, you or someone you know may be in this same situation. One of two things will happen in the end. Do not let the possibility of failure prevent you from believing God. Do not give up; do not give in, embrace Jesus and His word. Opposition is resistance, and resistance builds strength. Strength is power, and power is the energy behind any force. The goal of opposition is to help us to focus, to eliminate non-essentials and to devote ourselves to the essentials. It will cause the truly devoted to work harder which will make them stronger. Have the courage to believe and act upon the Word of God. Remember a hero is simply a person that went just one step beyond everyone else.

✢

PRAYER: Make a commitment to not be afraid.

MEMORIZE & MEDITATE: Psalms 27:1

FAITH ACTION: Confess your will to live to someone else.

Your word will not depart from my heart!

Appointed
TO
Triumph

CHAPTER EIGHT

He will *shield* you with his wings.

He will shelter YOU with his feathers.

His *faithful* promises are your

armor and PROTECTION.

Psalms 91:4 (NLT)

My Confession

Being confident, sure and firm in the fact that God began a good work in me, He will make sure that my work is finished before the day of Christ Jesus' return. He shall cover me with His feathers, and under His wings I shall take refuge; His truth shall be my shield and buckler. God is my refuge and strength and ever present help through my current troubles. I know He is with me always, even to the end of my life. He is my God. He will strengthen me and help me. He will uphold me with His righteous right-hand. Jesus is with me in weakness, and in fear, and in much trembling. My faith stands not in the wisdom of man, but in the power of God.

✢

PHILIPPIANS 1:6 · PSALMS 91:4 · PSALMS 46:1

MATTHEW 28:20 · ISAIAH 41:10; 1

Appointed To Triumph

When you think about the Christian lifestyle, it really is an unfair advantage toward anyone in any circumstance that is not a believer. It is like playing cards with a stacked deck, or buying stock with inside trader information. In other words you really have to work hard to fail. Yet all around us we see Christians struggling just to make it through life. Life seems to hand them one set-back after another. They can never gain victory. Why?

I suppose there is more than one simple reason, but I wish to give my thoughts. People have no problem believing they were saved FROM sin and judgment but struggle to believe they are saved FOR an everlasting life. When does eternal life begin for the Christian? Not when we get to heaven but when we receive Jesus Christ into our lives. Think of it this way; would a wealthy billionaire invest everything he owns on a single investment and then walk away and leave that investment to find its own way to success? No! Then why would God give up His only Son only to abandon you now? He did not and He would not. The problem then does not lie with God but with man. He wants one thing, and that is to be believed. Just look what He has done for you to live in this life.

1. He began a work in you, so that tells us He has a plan.

2. He intends to finish the construction.

3. He covers and shields us during the building process.

4. God is our safe haven and strength.

5. He is always there for us when troubles arise.

6.   He is continually making us stronger.

7.   He is there to help us when we are not strong enough.

8.   He sustains us with His own strength.

9.   When we are afraid He is still with us.

"Our faith stands not in the wisdom of man, but in the power of God". This statement could be the difference between abundant life and constant disappointments. If we do not obey and practice the teaching and principles of the Word of God, then by our actions we prove our faith in the "wisdom of man". We sometimes disobey the Holy Spirit inside our heart or our conscience by making decisions we know are wrong. We then expect and even pray for God to bless our poor choices. It just cannot work that way. Our conscience sometimes leads us in a way we do not understand, but through prayer we can often confirm the will of God on a matter. If we put our faith in man's wisdom, that is all you will receive. Action toward God's Word and principles make the above 9 statements a reality.

✚

PRAYER: Thank God for His wisdom and plan for your life.

MEMORIZE & MEDITATE: Philippians 1:6

FAITH ACTION: Follow the Holy Spirit in you and confirm God's will through prayer.

Be still and know that I am God!

Troubles

WITHOUT BEING

Troubled

CHAPTER NINE

Come TO ME, ALL OF YOU WHO ARE WEARY AND

CARRY HEAVY BURDENS, AND I WILL GIVE YOU REST.

TAKE MY *yoke* UPON YOU. LET ME TEACH YOU,

BECAUSE I AM HUMBLE AND *gentle,*

AND YOU WILL *find* REST FOR YOUR SOULS.

Matthew 11:28-30 (NLT)

My Confession

I come and offer to Jesus the heaviness of my struggles to understand my situation, and the burden of having to walk through them, and I exchange them for His rest, comfort and peace. I receive and bind myself to Jesus to learn from Him: for He is meek, gentle, and lowly of heart, and I will find rest for my soul in Him. For He harnesses me to things that are easy, and burdens me with things that are light. I have decided to remain and survive, in Jesus, and allow His words to be deposited in me, so that when I will ask Him whatever I desire, it shall be done for me. By this the Father is glorified, that I bear much fruit, reproducing the likeness of Christ in my body; it is in this that I show the world I am his disciple.

MATTHEW 11:28-30 · JOHN 15:7,8

TROUBLES WITHOUT BEING TROUBLED

Let's settle one thing first; Jesus never promised a life without difficulties. He did, however, offer us a way whereby we could go through them and yet not have the devastating effect that it has on most people. Read what Jesus said, "...*in me you may have peace. In this world you will have trouble. But take heart! I have overcome the world.*" John 16:33. During this fight we are going through with my wife's health, it has sounded like a broken record when visitors come into our home, "There is real peace here". Even when we go to the hospital, workers comment on how we seem so calm about everything. In public people cannot believe our attitude. How is this possible? What did we do? What should you do?

⊛   Come to Jesus.

⊛   Offer, and give to Jesus your burden.

⊛   Give and release to Him the question of "why".

⊛   Receive His comfort and peace.

⊛   Drawer closer than ever to Jesus.

⊛   Decide to be teachable by the Holy Spirit.

⊛   Allow Him to carry the burden by choosing not to worry about the future, because you cannot control it anyway.

⊛   Make up your mind that you will win over your problem.

⊛   Understand the Word of God concerning your situation.

⊛   Ask Him to help you bring His word into reality in your circumstance.

⊛   Know that God desires His glory in your life.

⦿   He wants to use you to reveal Christ to others.

It may not seem like it, but you have before you one of the greatest opportunities in your life. The creator of the universe desires for you come close enough to Him that He will actually exchange your problem for His peace. That is what communion is; the spiritual union between your heart and God's Spirit. Even communion with God does not make the problem go away, but helps you see that there is more to life than what you are currently experiencing. As time goes by and you look back, you will have discovered that real life is knowing, living, and abiding in Christ. God desires fellowship with you above the life of His own Son Jesus. You see, He sacrificed His own life in order that you could experience what He has known for all eternity, that God loves you and wants you more than any thing else. A way has been provided in order for you not just to get through it, but overcome it. Yes, God desires you to be victorious over it. The answer, though, is in Him, not about Him. Draw close to Him now.

☩

PRAYER: Give up your burden.

MEMORIZE & MEDITATE: Matthew 11:28

FAITH ACTION: QUIT WORRYING.

For you are Great and Mighty!

THE Lord is, He will

CHAPTER TEN

May the *Lord* BLESS you and PROTECT you.

May the lord smile on YOU and be gracious

to you. May the lord show you his *favor*

and GIVE you His PEACE.

Numbers 6:24-26 (NLT)

My Confession

"The Lord is blessing me and remaining with me; the Lord is making the glory of His face to shine upon me, and He is being gracious, and compassionate to me; the Lord is lifting up His countenance and expression upon me, and giving me peace, healing and prosperity." For He has said to me, "I will restore health to you, and I will heal your wounds", for He is the Lord, my God, who takes hold of my right hand and says to me, "Do not fear, I will help you". Surely God is my help; the Lord is the one who sustains and keeps me going. I will go in the strength of the LORD my God; therefore, I cast all my cares on the Lord for He is sustaining and assisting me.

✠

NUMBERS 6:24-26 · JEREMIAH 30:17 · ISAIAH 41:13

PSALMS 54:4 · PSALMS 71:16 · PSALMS 55:22

THE *L*ORD IS, *H*E WILL

The fact that the scripture says "God is" implies an absolute. That "He will" implies His determination to complete something. But if we are talking about our lives we must realize this; we must become partners with God in this method. Our role is to simply believe, obey and wait. More dreams and visions are aborted prematurely because people give up or refuse to submit to God's principles. Patience is the one ingredient added to faith that causes dreams to become realities. God has nothing to do with a man's failure in life. Just look what He is doing in you and wants to complete.

- He is blessing you.
- He is with you.
- The magnificence of His person reflects on you.
- He is continually giving what you do not deserve.
- He does not give you what you truly deserve.
- He desires you to have peace, healing and prosperity
- He is healing things that have hurt you in the past.
- He is teaching you courage, yet helping you.
- He is the energy that allows you not to quit.
- You are developing strength like His.
- He is supporting you; your greatest cheerleader.
- He is watching your back at all times.

Imagine your circumstance and situation in life right now. Regardless of what you

currently see, know that God is actively working to manifest the above things in your life. The battle is not the war; the inning is not the game. Regardless of where you are, if you are still alive it is not over for you. Life and circumstances can change to conform to the 12 things mentioned. You are a part of a worldwide vision to establish the kingdom of God in the earth. God desires to show the people in the world who and what He really is. The world no longer needs to simply just hear about God, but to see and experience Him in His fullness. You are a single stone in that complete building. God is doing the same thing differently in others lives in order to establish the complete and total demonstration of Himself on earth. So having understood that, realize that blessing, health, prosperity, and strength are not just for and about you; it is always for the sake of others. Ultimately God desires you to redistribute the very things you have received from Him. You may quite possibly be the only Jesus that neighbor, co-worker, and family member ever see. Don't quit now.

PRAYER: Thank the Lord for His blessing.

MEMORIZE & MEDITATE: Psalms 55:22

FAITH ACTION: Daily confess out loud these 12 truths.

My soul thirsts, it longs for you!

Prayer
MORE THAN ASKING TO
Receive

CHAPTER ELEVEN

All THAT'S REQUIRED IS THAT

YOU REALLY *believe* AND DO

NOT DOUBT IN *your* HEART.

Mark 11:23-24 (NLT)

My Confession

I am not anxious or stressed out, but by my prayers and specific requests, with thanksgiving, I make my appeals known to God; and the peace of God, which surpasses all understanding, continues to guard my heart and my mind through Christ Jesus. My prayer of faith will heal sickness, and the Lord will raise me up. I know that whatever things I ask in prayer, believing, I will receive whatever I request. Before I call out my request, He will answer; and while I am still speaking, He will hear me. When I call to Him He will answer me and show me great and mighty things that I do not yet have knowledge of. I do know this though, that if it depends on me, it is impossible, but not with God: for with Him all things are possible. Therefore I say to sickness and disease, "be removed from my body"; I do not doubt at all but I believe in what I ask for. I further believe that I have received full restoration of health in my body which is the dwelling place of the Holy Spirit.

ISAIAH 65:24 · JAMES 5:15 · MATTHEW 21:22 · MARK 11:23, 24

PHILIPPIANS 4:6,7 · JEREMIAH 33:3 · MATTHEW 21:22

PRAYER, MORE THAN ASKING TO RECEIVE

Sometimes we are so consumed by our needs and problems we forget the other benefits of prayer. God is not the big Santa Claus in the sky waiting for our list of requests so He may determine which He will grant and those He will deny. He is not a Father that is too busy for His children and only has time to grant their wishes and needs. Although as mentioned in the confessional, He desires that we tell Him about our needs and requests. Prayer is a training ground where-by we can learn some of life's greatest lessons.

What prayer can teach us:

1. To release stress and anxiety.

2. Teach us to be thankful.

3. God is the first person we let our needs be known to.

4. To guard our heart and mind with his peace.

5. To pray in faith for miraculous medical recoveries.

6. Teaches us to believe in what we do not currently see.

7. That God is already aware of our future.

8. For you to realize that He is always listening to you.

9. He wants to give you an answer outside your pre-conceived way of thinking.

10. Teach you that He is the God of the impossible.

11. To speak direct change to your circumstance.

12.   Teach you to never doubt what you speak.

13.   To understand He wants to fully restore your health.

14.   That the Holy Spirit lives inside you.

Anything on this list you need? By continually spending time in prayer you will find yourself changing. This is influence; you will become like the people you spend the most time with; they have the power to sway and persuade. God is an influencer, and you learn His ways through time with Him. Hypocrisy or stage acting is when you try to imitate through knowledge, while true faith is when you are influenced by the personal relationship. Influence then is not what we know, rather who we know. Prayer is the forum God uses to reveal Himself to us personally and intimately. It is the communication of our spirit with the Holy Spirit. Prayer is not a one-sided conversation; the Lord desires to speak into our spirit by His Spirit and through His Word. Prayer is also where we learn to listen. It seems whenever we come to God we have an agenda. God really only has one thing on His list — you. He desires time with you. Make yourself available to Him, and watch you and your circumstances change.

✢

PRAYER: Ask God to commune with you.

MEMORIZE & MEDITATE: Philippines 4:6, 7

FAITH ACTION: Plan for daily, uninterrupted time with God.

My fortress, my deliver!

a Real life

PARTNER

CHAPTER TWELVE

PEOPLE WITH *their* MINDS SET ON YOU.

you KEEP COMPLETELY WHOLE. STEADY

ON THEIR FEET, BECAUSE THEY KEEP

AT IT AND DON'T *quit*.

Isaiah 26:3 (NLT)

My Confession

I trust in, rely on, and have confidence toward the Lord with all my heart which is the source of my courage. I am not supported by my own understanding and insight; in everything I do, I recognize, perceive and know by experience the Lord my God, and He shall direct my way of living, and how I travel forward in life so as to arrive at the destination He has predetermined for me by His Word. I know His reputation, fame, and glory and have decided I will put my hope and trust in God my Father. You, Lord, have not forsaken or abandoned those who search for you. The Lord is good to me, a place of protection and safety in the day of distress and trouble; the Lord knows I have trusted in Him. He continually keeps me in perfect peace, because my mind is focused on and directed toward Jesus because I love and trust in Him.

✠

PROVERBS 3:5,6 · PSALMS 9:10 · NAHUM 1:7

ISAIAH 26:3

A REAL LIFE PARTNER

A partner is somebody who takes part in an activity or undertaking with somebody else. The great thing about having God as a partner is that He becomes everything we lack or need to live a successful life. Even though we receive Christ into our life, He views our partnership just a little differently. He said… *"You did not choose me, but I chose you and appointed you to go and bear fruit — fruit that will last. Then the Father will give you whatever you ask in my name"* John 15:16. He picked you because you have something special and unique to offer the world. But in order for a successful partnership to work, each person must function in their proper capacity.

What God requires of you:

- Trust in, rely on, and have confidence in Him.

- 100% effort is required.

- Realize God sustains you; not your own wisdom.

- Accept the fact that God is working behind the scenes in all circumstances to direct your life for the future.

- Come to know Him in such a way that you expect and anticipate good things.

- Pursue Christ the person for personal security.

- Understand that even when you have troubles in life, He wants to protect you.

- Prove your love and commitment to the partnership by keeping your mind focused on Him so that His peace can guide you.

The interesting thing about these 8 requirements is that we are not asked to *perform* or *do* something for God. He wants to do for us, yet we must exercise these things to enable Him to work on our behalf. Another meaning for the word partner is a nautical one; it means… the timbers on a ship underneath the deck that are used to support the mast. Generally this is used as the word "partners". So "partners" are not a visible part of the vessel yet bear the weight of the device used to catch the energy that propels the craft. That is what God wants to be for you; foundational reinforcement in your life. Without Him we unnecessarily subject ourselves to things that, though intended for good, will damage us or slow down the progress toward our destination. Take time to develop and strengthen that relationship. Do not allow outside forces to prevent you from that priority. You cannot afford to have a casual relationship with God if you want to realize all your hopes and dreams. Time alone with God should be the most important priority in your day. So make time for God; without it failure is unavoidable.

✢

PRAYER: Ask God to help you in this partnership.

MEMORIZE & MEDITATE: Isaiah 26:3

FAITH ACTION: Act on God's word, not your own wisdom.

Strong, bold and courageous!

Cause AND Effect

CHAPTER THIRTEEN

They DO NOT FEAR BAD NEWS; THEY

CONFIDENTLY TRUST THE LORD TO CARE FOR

THEM. THEY ARE *confident* AND FEARLESS

AND CAN FACE THEIR FOES TRIUMPHANTLY.

Psalms 112:7 (NLT)

My Confession

I will not be afraid of horrible and unpleasant news. My heart is resolute and committed, trusting in Jesus. He causes me to hear His loving-kindness in the morning, for I trust in Him. He causes me to know and make the right decisions, and so I lift up my soul to the Lord. I pay attention to and take notice of God's Word, and in doing so I have found prosperity and success in all that I do. I trust in the Lord my God, and therefore I am blessed; but even when I am afraid, I will put my confidence in God my Father. I believe in your loving-kindness and faithfulness towards me. My inner person rejoices in my future deliverance from this trouble. Judge and examine my life, Lord, for I have walked in Your godly character and integrity. I have trusted in You without hesitation.

PSALMS 112:7 · PSALMS 143:8 · PROVERBS 16:20

PSALMS 13:5 · PSALMS 26:1

CAUSE AND EFFECT

A cause is something that makes something else happen. An effect is what happens because of the cause. The cause is when I put my glasses on, the effect is that I can see better. In life we run into "causes" that are not of our choosing. Yet this law still comes into play. "Your wife has a tumor, and it is cancerous", is what my wife's doctor told me on March 4th, 2005. That "cause" set about a chain reaction of things; the disease caused something else to happen. However, the effect is not like the cause according to the Word of God. We can determine what happens, not because of the "cause" but because of what the Word of God says. What should our reaction be to such "causes"?

- Do not be afraid.
- Remain firmly committed to Christ.
- Listen for His reaction, especially early in the morning.
- Respond to and obey whatever He says.
- Pour out your emotions to the Lord.
- Discover what God's Word has to say about it.
- Obey that Word and expect positive results.
- Your faith and trust result in blessing.
- Continue to believe even when fear comes.
- Believe in His love and faithfulness toward you.
- Be happy for the positive outcome in the future.
- Continue to be a person of integrity and do not allow bitterness.

Even the "effect" of cancer does not have to cause death in my wife's body; God's Word is a higher law. But the effect of God's law only comes into reality if we choose to believe it and incorporate it into our daily living. Faith moves God to action; unbelief ties His hands. Your "cause" will make something else happen; either you will respond and believe the Word of God or you will not. The "effect" or end result then is one of choice. Sometimes we can be overwhelmed by our circumstance; find someone to help you through it, preferably someone who has walked where you are walking. Allow your faith to grow; even as it is developing, God's grace will sustain you. Do not be ashamed or discouraged by where you are at in faith; rather strengthen it by hearing and then believing God's Word. Like exercising your muscles it take persistence and time to develop strength, but you have to get started.

✣

PRAYER: Talk honestly to God about your situation.

MEMORIZE & MEDITATE: Proverbs 16:20

FAITH ACTION: Release your anxiety.

His love endures forever!

God *the* Caregiver

CHAPTER FOURTEEN

I WILL BE YOUR *God* THROUGHOUT YOUR

LIFETIME — UNTIL YOUR HAIR IS WHITE WITH AGE.

I *made* YOU. AND I WILL CARE FOR YOU.

I WILL CARRY YOU ALONG AND *save* YOU.

Isaiah 46:4 (NLT)

My Confession

I am not scared or afraid, for you are with me; I am not looking at and gazing upon my trouble or disappointment, for you are my God. You have made me courageous and brave and reinforced me; yes, you have helped and sustained me; yes, you are continuing to grasp and hold on to me and defend me with the right hand of your righteousness and justice. Just as a mother comforts and reassures, so you are soothing and calming me; even when I am of old age, You are the One; and when my hair turns gray You will still be carrying and holding me. You have fashioned me to be productive, and You are supporting, and sustaining me; yes, You will deliver me and cause me to escape my current trouble.

✛

ISAIAH 41:10 · ISAIAH 66:13 · ISAIAH 46:4

God The Care Giver

Regardless of our age or maturity God is still our Father. A father is one who brings up and looks after a child. Bringing us up is to nurture, train, and educate us for abundant living. To look after is — to be responsible, concerned, and be affectionate towards someone. At a certain age I was convinced my Dad was the dumbest human being on the planet. Reflecting back, I know his hard lessons for me were to train me for life. Regardless of our maturity God is always moving us forward, training us for our future. Although things seem strange and His ways ridiculous, we have to allow Him to be our Father.

He is training and educating you as your Father

- His presence is with you, so there is no need to be scared.
- Look directly at Him, not your trouble.
- He is making you stronger — a person of courage.
- He wants to help and assist you.
- He is molding you to be beneficial to your world.

He is affectionate and concerned about you

1. He is persistent with you, never giving up.
2. He will defend and guard you.
3. He comforts you in weakness and failure.
4. He reassures you when you become tense and upset.

5. He will carry and hold you when you get old and needy.

6. He is your #1 fan and cheerleader.

7. He gets you out of the mess you cannot get out of alone.

It is important to understand that it is because you are God's child that He loves you. Pure love is not relying on the same response before it acts. I love my children and do not wait for their approval or consent to interact in their lives. Even if they do not understand or believe that I am acting on their behalf for their good, I do it anyway. If they misinterpret my decisions as being mean and hindering their lives, I will stand by those decisions and still love them. If they choose to rebel, it does not change my affection and concern for them in the least. As a parent I am still prone to make mistakes, just like your parents; but God the Father is not. Remember the command *"children obey your parents"*, there is no clause stating parents obey your children. God is our Father; submit to His ways, receive His affection, and trust Him and His wisdom.

✦

PRAYER: Ask God to reveal himself as a Father to you.

MEMORIZE & MEDITATE: Isaiah 41:10

FAITH ACTION: Decide to obey God's ways.

Trust in the Lord with all your heart!

God YOUR friend

CHAPTER FIFTEEN

I WILL GIVE YOU *peace* IN THE LAND,

AND YOU WILL BE ABLE TO SLEEP WITHOUT

FEAR. I WILL *remove* THE WILD

ANIMALS FROM YOUR LAND AND PROTECT

you FROM YOUR ENEMIES.

Leviticus 26:6 (NLT)

My Confession

I have called on you, and I have come and prayed to you, and you have listened and paid attention with great interest to me. I have come to you, with all my burdens, grief, and the heavy load of my sadness, and you have caused me to stop my own efforts in order for me to recover and collect my strength. You have granted me safety, health, and completeness on the earth now, not just later in heaven; you have caused me to recline and rest, and nothing or no one will startle me or make me afraid: you are initiating the living objects that are bad, unpleasant, and disagreeable to cease and come to an end on the earth for me, neither shall my enemy's weapons go through my habitation. I am returning to and revisiting all my natural family and you are with me. When I am of old age you will return to me and say, "Yes, I have loved you forever and always. With goodness, kindness, and faithfulness I have seized you and led you along all these years."

JEREMIAH 29:12 · MATTHEW 11:28 · LEVITICUS 26:6

GENESIS 31:3 · JEREMIAH 31:3

GOD YOUR FRIEND

I like my friends. They are people I can always depend on. They know my weaknesses and failures and don't care; they like me anyway. When I am angry, sad, exited, bored, passionate about the future, disgusted with the present and goofy, one common quality is consistent. In fact it is with anyone's friend — they are good listeners. I suppose if we could change the word "friend" it would have to be "listener". The Lord wants to be your friend (listener). Just look how the Bible describes Him.

- You can cry out and approach Him at will.
- He listens to you when you talk.
- He is keenly interested in what you have to say.
- He is interested in just you, who you are.
- You can dump all your emotions on Him.
- He wants to strengthen you.
- He is your source of safety, health, and fullness.
- He is one you can rest and relax with.
- You do not need to be afraid of anything.
- He is making the first move to rid your life of trouble.
- He is guarding your home from the devil's schemes.
- He promises to love you forever.
- He will always be gentle, kind and faithful to you.

God wants you to be His friend for the same reasons. Friendship is not one-sided;

THE *Lord* IS YOUR *Guardian*

CHAPTERSIXTEEN

On the VERY *day* I call to you for help, my

enemies will retreat. This I know: God is on my

side. O God. I PRAISE your *word*. I trust

in *God,* so why should I be AFRAID?

What can mere MORTALS do to me?

Psalms 56:9-11 (NLT)

My Confession

The very day I cried for help the tide of the battle turned. My enemies fled! This one thing I know, God is for me! I am trusting God – oh praise His promises! I am not afraid of anything mere man can do to me! Yes, praise His promises. He will surely do what He promised; Lord, thank you for your help. You have saved me from death and my feet from slipping, so that I can walk before you in the land of the living. You sent your word and healed me, and you delivered me so that I escaped from the grave. I will not die but live and declare to others how you desire to satisfy and fulfill them with long life, and how you will personally show them your welfare and prosperity.

✠

PSALMS 56:9-13 · PSALMS 107:20 · PSALMS 118:17

PSALMS 91:16

THE LORD IS YOUR GUARDIAN

The word guardian is a legal term that means somebody who is legally appointed to look after the affairs of another. When you made the decision to receive Christ into your life, He became your legal guardian. Not a self-appointed guardian, not by your will, but a guardian established by the judicial system that governs the universe. A guardian, therefore, has certain responsibilities that if not followed through on can come under the judgment of the court. God holds Himself accountable to His Word or faces judicial consequences. Because it is impossible for God to lie, or to fail to perform His duty as a legal guardian, it is up to us to yield our lives to his Lordship. Whether or not He will be our guardian is our choice.

The advantages of God as your legal guardian:

1. We can cry out to God when we are in trouble.

2. God can change our circumstance when we cannot.

3. Our enemy knows Him and is afraid of Him.

4. We know by experience that God wants us to succeed.

5. We learn success comes from our trust in Him.

6. As we trust we learn to praise Him for our future.

7. We are not afraid of people and what they can do.

8. We are sure that God will do what He says in His Word.

9. We become a grateful person.

10.   He protects our life and life's journey from harm.

11.   We can walk through this life with God's favor.

12.   His Word heals and rescues us from trouble.

13.   We find a greater purpose to life than what we can get.

14.   We show others the abundant life God has for them too.

Imagine walking through life with God and His designated angels as your bodyguards. When we see people with an entourage of guards, or the secret service's protection, we know that person is someone important and of great worth. It also indicates that person has enemies that would like to harm or destroy them. When we fail to yield to the Lordship of Christ, we lose our protection. We become an unguarded target for our enemy. Our future benefit to others is now in jeopardy. Some people think God is legally bound to protect us regardless of what we do. Doing our own thing is proof we are not trusting God. Fear is evidence that we are outside His guardianship. We can be under His protection immediately simply by crying out to Him for help. *"Whoever calls upon the name of the Lord will be saved"*.

✢

PRAYER: Ask God to show you what is not under His Lordship in your life

MEMORIZE & MEDITATE: Psalms 56:9

FAITH ACTION: Repent by confession and by changing those areas of your life God convicts you of.

I place before you life and death, choose life!

Life's Choices

TODAY I HAVE *given* YOU A CHOICE BETWEEN LIFE

AND DEATH, BETWEEN **BLESSINGS** AND CURSES. I CALL

ON *heaven* AND EARTH TO WITNESS THE CHOICE

YOU MAKE. OH THAT YOU WOULD CHOOSE **LIFE**, THAT

YOU AND **YOUR** DESCENDANTS MIGHT *live!*

Deuteronomy 30:19 (NLT)

My Confession

I will hold firmly to the confession of my hope that it is "by the whipping Jesus received and the blood loss and bruising that occurred as a result, sickness and disease is forever removed from my body". I will be stubborn and unmoved by this fact. For you are the one who promised, and you are faithful. You assured me that while I am on earth anything that I will ask, it will be done for me by you, Father, who resides in heaven. You have set before me life and death, the blessing and the curse: I CHOOSE LIFE, and I will live, me and my family.

HEBREWS 10:23 · 1 PETER 2:24 · MATTHEW 18:19

DEUTERONOMY 30:19

LIFE'S CHOICES

Ever noticed how much blame the devil gets for life's failures? Even God is at fault, while the last place we seem to look at is in the mirror. Remember the cause and effect principle we spoke of earlier? Our choices, good and bad, determine almost all our future circumstances. The goal is to make the right choices, because the devil is real and is out to destroy us anyway. We do not need to help him out by making wrong decisions. When we make the right choices according to the will and Word of God we position our future for blessing and increase. To choose the life of blessing is to choose the lifestyle God requires. You cannot live in deliberate sin and rebellion toward God's Word and expect God's blessing. A Christian is not a person that prays a prayer and goes to church. A Christian is a follower, a student, and practitioner of God's Word.

What can a follower of Christ expect out of life?

1. Hope for our future by our confession of the Word.
2. God to manifest His promises to us on earth.
3. Continually experience the dependability of God.
4. Assurance of answered prayer.
5. Heaven's experiences can come to earth by asking.
6. Choices for good and bad things in life.
7. Ability to choose between good and bad beforehand.
8. The wisdom to make the right decision every time.

9.   To experience a blessed life on earth.

10.   For our family to experience a blessed life on earth.

When we make bad choices God has established a mechanism whereby we can get back into the blessing lifestyle. It's called repentance. It means to turn and go the opposite direction. We sometimes confuse God's forgiveness with our repentance. People who do not change behavior but want forgiveness are simply sorry they got caught. They want to feel better today and then never change their lifestyle. This is when we begin blaming everyone and everything else but ourselves. *"Do not be deceived, God cannot be mocked, a man reaps what he sows"* Galatians 6:7. In other words, do not be tricked into thinking it was God's fault because your wrong actions produced negative results. Confess your bad choices, ask forgiveness, and then make the decision not to make them again. Enlist the help of others if you need to. My point is not to dwell on our shortcomings, rather get us on the right track to God's very best for our life. Remember you can choose blessing over any curse. Make the right choice starting today.

✛

PRAYER: Ask God to reveal bad choices you have made that currently are affecting your life in a negative way.

MEMORIZE & MEDITATE: Deuteronomy 30:19

FAITH ACTION: Make whatever lifestyle changes are necessary.

My thoughts are not your thoughts!

What
ARE YOU *Thinking?*

CHAPTER EIGHTEEN

PAY ATTENTION, MY *child,* TO WHAT I SAY.

LISTEN CAREFULLY. DON'T LOSE SIGHT OF MY WORDS.

LET THEM PENETRATE DEEP WITHIN YOUR *heart,*

FOR THEY BRING *life* AND RADIANT HEALTH TO

ANYONE WHO DISCOVERS THEIR MEANING.

Proverbs 4:20-22 (NLT)

My Confession

Father as your child, I will pay attention and keep my mind on your words. I choose to turn my ear to listen to what you are personally saying to me. I will not let what you speak to me depart from my mental and spiritual senses. I will keep them in the forefront and center of my inner person, my will, and my place of courage; for they are life to me when I find them and health to my whole body. I will guard and fortify the knowledge and the understanding of your word in order to protect my future health and prosperity. Out of your words and promises are my complete sources of life on the earth.

✠

PROVERBS 4:20-23

What Are You Thinking?

Action follows thought; we think it then we do it. Good or bad behavior can be controlled by what goes through our mind. If we change what we think about, behavior will eventually do the same. What do you read, and watch on TV? What do you talk about? What are you thinking as you drive your car? If it were possible to do a "thought inventory" on people to study behavior, I would imagine we would discover an amazing link. Most of us would not think that we have a thought problem and that may be true. But are we all satisfied with our behavior and character? Probably not; yet if we can agree on the idea that thought could control behavior, then it is safe to say that if we discipline our mind toward the positive and the Godly attributes, our behavior would follow.

How can we control our thoughts?

- Focus on and think on God's Word as much as we can.

- Choose to eliminate distracting thoughts.

- Position our minds to hear the Holy Spirit.

- When we hear and understand the Word of God, use whatever tools needed to remember it.

- Memorize the Word of God.

- Discipline your mind to meditate on the Word.

- Recognize evil thoughts and renounce them.

How to evaluate thoughts to make good decisions:

1. Recall the Word before making important decisions.

2. Allow God's Word to give you faith in your decisions.

3. Godly wisdom is peaceful and stress free.

4. Protect yourself from stress and anxiety by reinforcing and confirming your decisions according to the Word.

5. Be confident that your obedience to the Word will produce the result.

I sometimes wish God had a magic pill that could correct and change my behavior. Other than using pain from failure to change behavior, His Word meditated on and put to practice will change me. Read what God tells the most successful military leader in history. *"Do not let this book of the law depart from your mouth, meditate on it day and night, so that you may be careful to do everything that is written in it. THEN you will be prosperous and successful"* Joshua 1:8. Meditation is the emptying of the mind of thoughts, or concentration of the mind on just one thing, in order to aid mental or spiritual development. Meditation produces understanding, understanding produces confidence for action. Acting on the word of God as a result of understanding IS faith. God always rewards obedient faith with prosperity and success.

✟

PRAYER: Ask God how you are feeding your mind that affects negative behavior.

MEMORIZE & MEDITATE: Proverbs 4:23

FAITH ACTION: Make a commitment to God to meditate on His Word daily.

The magnificence of His sacrifice!

THE *Blood* OF *Christ*

CHAPTER NINETEEN

For god sent *Jesus* to take the punishment

for our sins and to SATISFY god's anger against us.

We are made right with *God* when we believe that

jesus SHED his blood, SACRIFICING his life for us.

Romans 3:25 (NLT)

My Confession

For you say to me, "This is my blood of the new covenant, the agreement or treaty, which is poured out for many". God sent Jesus into the world to be the sacrifice, to atone, and pay the cost for my crimes. Through the conviction of this truth, it is in your shed blood, that you show me your righteousness, the right way I should be before you, because you now ignore my previous sins by your mercy. The very existence of life in my body is in my blood, and you have given me your blood on the altar to make atonement for and to cover my complete person: for it is your blood that covers and coats me with your life.

MARK 14:24 · ROMANS 3:25 · LEVITICUS 17:11

THE *B*LOOD OF *C*HRIST

Blood is the fluid that circulates in a person's heart, arteries, capillaries and veins, carrying nourishment and oxygen to and taking waste products from all parts of the body. Blood fights against infection and helps heal wounds. There is no long term substitute for human blood.

As I am writing I am looking on the wall of my office, and I can see a picture of Jesus wearing the crown of thorns with blood running down his face. Leviticus 17 says…*The very existence of life in our bodies is in our blood.*

What is the significance of the blood of Christ?

1. It established a new treaty between God and man.
2. God sent Jesus into the world to bleed and become the substitute for God's judgment for our crimes against Him.
3. It was the price that God's law demanded to forgive sin.
4. Only an innocent person's blood could substitute for ours.
5. It proves that Christ was completely righteous and holy before God.
6. Judgment is removed from our life and the righteous and holy life of Christ is given to us instead.
7. We do not receive what we deserve; punishment, eternal death and separation from God.
8. Jesus gave the very existence of His eternal life to us.

9. His blood now covers over us as a reminder to God that we are Holy and Righteous just as He was on the earth.

10. The life that Christ had on earth, His relationship with God the Father is the same life we can now enjoy.

There is no greater truth, doctrine or revelation in the Bible than to understand what you have just read. There is nothing more important that the devil would like to keep you ignorant of than the understanding of the blood of Christ. The blood of Christ destroyed the devil's kingdom. It has restored you into right relationship with God the Father. God does not need to do anything else to appease His law for man's transgression. We are not just delivered from the penalty of sin — Jesus took away the power of sin in us. We are not saved from sin and that is the end of the story. We are given Christ's life in exchange. Resist the attitude that you do not deserve such a wonderful gift. God has already given you what you do not deserve. He is offering it to you today; accept it with a grateful heart. Get the book "The Power of the Blood of Christ" by Andrew Murray; no greater book has ever been written on this subject.

✟

PRAYER: Thank God for His substitute for your sin.

MEMORIZE & MEDITATE: Romans 3:25

FAITH ACTION: Allow Christ life to control you.

My redeemer lives!

Redeemed *Life* For Life

CHAPTER TWENTY

JUST THINK *how* MUCH MORE THE BLOOD OF CHRIST

WILL PURIFY OUR HEARTS FROM DEEDS THAT LEAD TO

DEATH SO THAT WE CAN *worship* THE LIVING GOD.

FOR BY THE POWER OF THE ETERNAL SPIRIT, CHRIST

OFFERED *himself* TO GOD AS A PERFECT

SACRIFICE FOR OUR SINS. *Hebrews 9:14* (NLT)

My Confession

I know that I was released from the penalty of sin by reason of a ransom; the payment being the precious, esteemed, and honorable blood of a lamb without any fault before God whatsoever-the blood of you, Jesus our Christ; For indeed Christ, my Passover lamb saved me from eternal death, having been sacrificed in my place. It is you, Jesus, with the help of the Holy Spirit who is without beginning, that gave yourself over to God the Judge as a man without blame or fault in your life. How much greater then will your blood free me from my faults in order that I can tell the difference between what is morally good and bad and from what are spiritually lifeless acts and deeds in order to serve you, the living God? For you Jesus said, "It is finished" when you died on the cross, signifying the liberation of my soul.

✝

1 PETER 1:18-19 · 1 CORINTHIANS 5:7

HEBREWS 9:14 · JOHN 19:30

REDEEMED FOR LIFE

Generally when we think of the word ransom we think about kidnappers demands for holding a hostage. You have seen the movies when the bad guy thinks he can make some big money, so he kidnaps a rich person's relative, holds them against their will, then notifies the wealthy relative and threatens to kill the hostage if the demands are not met. The exception would be when the kidnapped person becomes one of the bad guys and begins to inflict the original kidnappers terror on others (Patty Hearst story). Using that thought should give clarity to Jesus' redemption of our souls. This is the scene and the characters…

- You are the hostage, held by sin and the devil.
- You have no way of escape, NONE.
- Without a rescue attempt you are going to die.
- This is not just physical death, but an eternal one.
- Your captors specialize in making life miserable.
- But now the law sees you as one of the kidnappers.
- You have to suffer the judgment for breaking the law.
- Someone decides to change places with you.
- They will suffer the penalty of death; you get to live.
- The law is satisfied, and you are pardoned.

Seems simple enough. What person would not do that? Some would say, "I am not worthy of such an exchange"; that is true. Some would say, "I can get out of this myself". But as you can see from the previous scenario, this is where the story

136

turns for the captor's worst. Not only is the captor held by sin and the devil, but the law of God now sees you as one of the criminals. The only way of escape is to allow Jesus Christ to become the substitute for us. That is not where the story ends, but it is where most Christians stop.

You see when Jesus became our substitute He took everything away from us that was bad and evil. We are no longer criminals under the law of God. He then gave us everything He possesses. We have nothing but sin and death. He takes that and it's penalty, and we get abundant life with all the blessings of Abraham on the earth today. Imagine what it must be like for a real criminal to be pardoned from his crimes. A person that had no hope until someone within the legal/judicial system came along and out of pure love says, "I will take your life, and you can have mine". That is what Jesus did for us! What's the catch? You must believe by faith that it is true. It is as if Jesus left a will at his death outlining our inheritance. It must be received in order for it to become activated.

✢

PRAYER: Thank God for providing for our ransom.

MEMORIZE & MEDITATE: Hebrews 9:14

FAITH ACTION: Accept God's abundant life.

With You, I can scale any wall!

You ARE A *Winner*

ALL PRAISE TO HIM WHO *loves*

US AND HAS FREED US FROM OUR SINS,

BY *shedding* HIS BLOOD FOR US.

Revelation 1:5 (NLT)

My Confession

"You are worth everything, Jesus, for you were killed, and purchased me for God with your blood; People out of every tribe, language, and nation; for you loved me, and washed me from my sins by your blood. I am carried off like a victorious champion because of the blood of Jesus, and I demonstrate to my enemy that I am more than a conqueror by the words of my mouth testifying of what you have personally done in my life. I will not love my own life, even unto death. Your blood shall also be for me a distinguishing mark on the house where I live, and there shall be no fatal strike on me to destroy or ruin my life.

REVELATION 1:5 · REVELATION 5:9 · REVELATION 12:11

EXODUS 12:13

YOU ARE A WINNER

What a big difference between the words "have won" and "will win". As Christians, Jesus already having won the victory over sin and death for us, declares us WINNERS. My friend Pastor Mickey Keith illustrates it this way. A conqueror is like a prize fighter who has trained, prepared, and worked his entire life for the goal of winning the championship. He has fought and defeated an opponent to claim that prize. Having won, he receives the prize money and the champion's belt for his victory. He comes home a crowned champion with the prize money, and his wife takes the check and says, "thank you". She is MORE than a champion! She did nothing to earn the championship but was in right relationship with the champion and therefore receives all the reward that he does. Jesus is our champion; we are MORE than champions. Read what He did for us.

Jesus — Our Champion

1. He died so we would not have to die.
2. He bought us out of sin by pouring out His blood for us.
3. No human on earth is exempt from becoming a potential champion.
4. He loves us as His own personal companion.
5. He makes us clean before God.
6. We are celebrated as champions because of our faith in Him and the work He did for us.
7. Our enemies know we are companions of the King and can never harm us again if we believe and confess with our mouth HIS victory!

8.   It is done for YOU, not just everyone else.

9.   Even when we physically die, we are still winners.

10. Jesus victory is final; no enemy can fight and defeat us in any way in this life.

We need to understand this last point. Just because bad things or disappointments happen in our life, it in no way means that our enemy has defeated us. We are only defeated if we quit, if we lose focus of who we truly are, winners in Christ. Remember, we have eternal life now and a battle is not the war. A single setback does not dictate our entire future. Our real future, our real purpose, our real destination is heaven. Heaven is the real prize and reward; an eternity spent without suffering or pain surrounded by the eternal life and presence of God our Father. Our enemy is the big loser. Separated and cast into an eternal lake of fire. So if the devil attempts to scare you or lie to you about your present circumstances, simply remind him of his future in hell and your future in heaven.

✢

PRAYER: Thank God for declaring you a champion.

MEMORIZE & MEDITATE: Revelation 1:5

FAITH ACTION: Begin to think, talk, and walk like the champion you really are in Christ.

Righteousness of God in Christ Jesus!

God's Declaration Of Righteousness

HE IS SO RICH IN *kindness*

THAT *he* PURCHASED OUR FREEDOM

THROUGH THE BLOOD OF HIS *Son,*

AND OUR SINS ARE *forgiven*.

Ephesians 1:7 (NLT)

My Confession

Now in you Jesus, I was once far from where you are, but you have made me close to you by your blood. Not only that, but you declared me just as righteous as you are before God by your blood, so now I am free from God's wrath and judgment. Your blood paid the ransom and penalty for my sin; you have forgiven me of my debt and pardoned me from further judgment, and you have filled my life with the abundance of your grace, joy and pleasure. I will walk in the truth of your word because that is where you are, and I will participate together with like-minded people, for your blood has and will continue to cleanse me from all sin.

EPHESIANS 2:13 · ROMANS 5:9 · 1 JOHN 1:7

EPHESIANS 1:7

GOD'S DECLARATION OF RIGHTEOUSNESS

In 1776 our forefathers signed the "Declaration of Independence". It was a document stating that America no longer would recognize England as its government; it would become its own sovereign nation, "independent" of the British. These men immediately became traitors in the eyes of the King, and war was soon to follow. Today for every man that would hear, God also has declared something to us. He announced it in the Good News of the Bible. In fact it is more than an announcement; it is a pro-nouncement upon everyone that will believe Him. What has He pronounced on us? That faith in His Son Jesus Christ's death and resurrection and the work that He performed on our behalf, if we believe it He declares us JUST AS RIGHTEOUS AS JESUS! That's right friend; you, me, sons and daughters of God. Look what else the Bible says about us.

- We are IN Jesus.
- We are close to Him now.
- We are declared righteous before God.
- We are free from God's wrath and judgment.
- God paid the debt of our ransom.
- Jesus suffered the penalty of sin for us.
- We owe and can never repay God.
- God will never look to inflict His wrath of judgment on us EVER.
- He causes our present life to overflow with things we do not deserve.
- He gives us happiness for life that is not controlled by present circumstances.

⦿ Our living produces a satisfaction and delight inside us that others do not have.

⦿ He has given us guidelines for living that cause us to maintain this type of lifestyle.

⦿ As we follow the Bible's guidelines we find that we are walking and living the way Christ lived.

⦿ He gives us friends that believe and structure their living just like we have ours.

⦿ His shed blood is a reminder to God that even our present sin is forgiven if we confess it to Him.

A lot of Bible truth is stated here! These are facts, but they only become functional if we choose to believe them. God has already pronounced you NOT GUILTY! But it did not stop there, He has also declared you RIGHTEOUS! Just believe it and accept it.

✢

PRAYER: Thank God for declaring you righteous.

MEMORIZE & MEDITATE: Romans 5:9

FAITH ACTION: Begin to think, talk, and walk like the child of God you really are.

I live to worship You!

No Quid Pro Quo

CHAPTER TWENTY THREE

He WAS WOUNDED AND CRUSHED FOR OUR SINS.

HE WAS BEATEN THAT WE MIGHT HAVE *peace*.

HE WAS *whipped*, AND WE WERE HEALED!

Isaiah 53: 5 (NLT)

My Confession

It was you, Lord Jesus, who was wounded, polluted, and defiled for my transgressions and rebellion; you were bruised and broken for my wickedness and evil; the punishment I deserved, you took for me; your death satisfied justice, and then you supplied me with completeness, health and prosperity; with your bruising and the wounds you suffered while being whipped, my body and soul is restored to complete and total health. While you were praying intensely and sincerely for me, your sweat became like great drops of blood falling down on the ground. Then your hands and feet were nailed to a cross. When you did this for me, you knew you would be intervening on my behalf in order to restore peace and friendship with God the Father. You then established a new arrangement whereby everything you possessed on the earth rightfully and legally became mine. Now I have freedom to speak before you in the holy place where you dwell by that same blood that you, Jesus, spilled on the earth.

ISAIAH 53:5 · LUKE 22:44 · PSALMS 22:16

HEBREWS 12:24 · HEBREWS 10:19

No Quid Pro Quo

Quid pro quo means something given or done in exchange for something else. In the Christian faith we must understand that quid pro quo can never be applied by man toward God. Jesus did not die and suffer expecting us to do something for Him to earn His mercy and grace. The truth is Jesus did everything for us; He took away our sentence of death and all its consequences and gave us His life and all its benefits. We stand unable to do a thing except believe these facts. This is what He did to take away our deserved punishment.

What Christ did for us

- He was ill-treated physically and mentally hurt.
- As an innocent man He was contaminated with our sin.
- His body was beaten and whipped unmercifully.
- He suffered lesions and cuts all over His body.
- His brain hemorrhaged, and He bled from His brow area from excessive stress.
- His naked body was nailed with spikes and hung on a wooden cross until He suffocated and died.
- He bled for over 12 straight hours as a result of the beating He received.

In turn we Received

1. God's own justice was satisfied when He died for us.

2. He gives us everything that is needed for complete health in our bodies and prosperity for our soul.

3. The peace and friendship God desired to have with us was re-established.

4. God gives to us everything Christ possessed on earth.

5. We have no restrictions placed on us to approach and speak to God.

Religion has crept into Christianity and somehow deceived us into thinking we have to "do" or "be" something to receive God's favor. When we attempt to "do" or "be" something to earn God's favor, we really cheapen and disrespect the work Christ did for us. The only thing God requires from us is that we love Him with everything we have. We "do", not to earn God's favor, rather to worship Him with our life. God loves us, period. He has proven that. Even your bad behavior and poor decisions cannot cause God to reject you. We cannot earn His love because He IS love. Believe He loves you and then receive His love towards you. Jesus suffered for you because He wants to bless, prosper, and change your life for the better. Let Him do it!

✢

PRAYER: Thank God for the love Jesus demonstrated toward you.

MEMORIZE & MEDITATE: Isaiah 53:5

FAITH ACTION: Live your life as an act of worship to God.

You are all I want in my life!

Intimacy
WITH
Christ

This *cup* is the new covenant between

God and you, sealed by the SHEDDING of

my blood. Do this in rememberance of me

as *often* as you drink it.

1 Corinthians 11:25, 26 (NLT)

My Confession

At your last meal before your death you spoke to your present and future followers and said, "This cup represents my blood, the new arrangement where-by everything I possess on the earth rightfully and legally became yours. Drink this often so as to make and produce memory of me and what I did for you". As often as I eat this bread, and drink this cup, I proclaim and declare your death and all that it accomplished for me until you return to the earth again. The cup of blessing which I celebrate is the intimate relationship I experience with you and of your blood, Lord Jesus. I eat of your flesh and drink of your blood and I have eternal life, and you will raise me up at the last day. I partake of your flesh and drink your blood, and so I live in you and you in me.

✢

1 CORINTHIANS 11:25, 26 · 1 CORINTHIANS 10:16

JOHN 6:54, 56

*I*NTIMACY WITH *J*ESUS

If you knew that you had 24 hours to live, what would you do? Jesus decided to have supper with His 11 closest friends. His last evening on earth, He took time to relax, eat, and impart His last requests to them. Of course later that evening, they all retreated to pray. The picture in this setting is that Jesus IS the center of attention, but He intimately and personally interacts with each man. All His friends also interact with each other. We imagine this as a very somber evening, even a depressing moment, but I think it was quite the opposite. It was the graduation ceremony for 11 men. Jesus was leaving earth and entrusting the future of the gospel to them. The things He did with them, and left for them, are applicable for us today.

1. A covenant agreement from Him towards us.
2. His earthly possessions are legally transferred to us.
3. The right to re-enact the meal in order to remember what He did for us.
4. Eating the meal publicly states that we acknowledge the substitutionary death of Christ until He returns.
5. We participate and celebrate our blessing from Him.
6. It reminds us of our intimate relationship with Christ.
7. The communion meal is a figurative representation of our unity with His death and His life.

When we partake of the figurative body and blood of our Lord, we are actually identifying ourselves with His death. Even greater, we are receiving and accepting

His life. The communion supper is our link to remembering all Christ did for us. It is a time of personal interaction and application of His life into our body, soul, and spirit. It is a time of celebration, not mourning. Christ gave us something we could never achieve on our own. It is cause for great joy and thanksgiving. It is a time to acknowledge His Lordship in our life and release all the failures and sin and allow those things to be released to Him through His death. We then have no cause to hold on to shame and disgrace any longer. As children of the Living God we hold our heads up high; we are confident of who we are. We come before Jesus with full assurance of faith. If we identify with Christ in this way, it makes us just as much a son of the Father as Jesus himself. Hebrews 2:11 says, "So Jesus is not ashamed to call them (us) brothers". Intimate relationship with Christ is not about being religious; rather it is about relaxing in God's presence while He imparts Himself into our lives.

✢

PRAYER: Ask Jesus to impart His life to you.

MEMORIZE & MEDITATE: Romans 5:1

FAITH ACTION: Take the communion supper today.

Fearfully and wonderfully made!

The *Security* Of Our *Father*

BECAUSE OF OUR *faith,* CHRIST HAS BROUGHT US

INTO THIS PLACE OF HIGHEST **PRIVILEGE** WHERE WE NOW

STAND, AND WE **CONFIDENTLY** AND *joyfully*

LOOK *forward* TO SHARING **GOD'S** GLORY.

Romans 5:2 (NLT)

My Confession

I have been pronounced honorably just, by conviction and trust in your word; I have peace and harmony with you, Father, through our Lord Jesus Christ; through Him I can now approach you because you accept me; I am firmly convinced that this is true; you gave me the right to your good will, loving-kindness and favor; in this position I stand firm, and I rejoice in expectation of even better things in the future together with the splendor and majesty of the Father. For no object or weapon formed and fashioned against me to do me harm shall be successful or advance, and every language and speech which rises against me as an act of deciding and shaping my future, you shall return the wickedness back to that enemy. This is the inheritance and possession of the servants and worshippers of the Lord. My righteousness is from YOU, because you said it is so.

✛

ROMANS 5:1, 2 · ISAIAH 54:17

THE SECURITY OF OUR FATHER

I have heard it said in the context of God our Father that "there is no such thing as an illegitimate child; there are only illegitimate parents". In other words, God is the creator of life. He has formed and fashioned every human being according to His own image. It is horrible that children should grow up without a father figure in their life. Yet throughout the New Testament the Bible refers to God as a father. The image He wants man to see of Himself is one of a daddy or a real Father. Since so many people today have never known what a real father is, look at how the Bible describes the attributes of God our Father and His affection toward them that receive Him.

The Affection of Our Father

- He says we are worthy of Him because we rely on Him.
- He is no longer in conflict and hostile towards us.
- We are in perfect union, joined together with Him.
- We can come into His presence.
- He affirms us as His children and is not angry with us.
- As children we are entitled to His favor, good will, and compassion.
- No enemy can use any device to gain advantage over us.
- Nothing anyone speaks over us can affect our future.
- If anyone tries to hurt us, they bring danger on themselves.
- Our inheritance is God's own righteousness.

Regardless of your experience and image of what a father is, God has defined what it really is. If He has defined it, then He is responsible to be it. He is not a bunch of talk and empty promises. He will perform. He is a Father, not a big Santa Claus in the sky waiting to grant our every wish. Because He loves us, He corrects us and disciplines us for our own future prosperity and success. Realize that He wants to be your Father, so relationship is a greater priority than your personal blessing. When we pursue Him not just the benefits of Him, we show and prove our love towards Him. We often confuse our unanswered requests to God as His being angry with us or even that He does not exist. The truth is, our pain or uncomfortable situation could be designed to force us to Him; not just for a solution or cure but to simply be with Him. Read how Paul describes Him; *"Because you are sons, God sent the Spirit of his Son into our hearts, the Spirit who calls out, "Abba, Father." So you are no longer a slave, but a son; and since you are a son, God has made you also an heir"* Galations 4:6-7. HE is our inheritance, NOT stuff and things. He IS our Papa, our Daddy; He is the one who sacrificed Jesus so we could have the same relationship with Him that Jesus has. What do you need to do to have this relationship? Simply believe in the substitutionary work of His Son.

✟

PRAYER: Thank God for being your Father.

MEMORIZE & MEDITATE: Romans 5:1

FAITH ACTION: Draw near to God because you love Him.

The mystery of the King...

You, Your,
You are

CHAPTER TWENTY SIX

THE LORD IS *merciful* AND GRACIOUS;

HE IS SLOW TO GET ANGRY AND

full OF UNFAILING LOVE.

Psalms 103: 8 (NLT)

My Confession

Your love, Lord, stretches and extends to and beyond all the galaxies. Your reliability can be counted on at all times; it covers me like a cloud in the sky. You are compassionate towards me and concerned about me. You bestow favor and kindness to me even though I am inferior to your greatness. Your face is slow to show the effects of anger, annoyance, and irritation towards me. Rather, you are always plenteous and abundant in good deeds regarding me. It is because of your great love and mercy for me that I am not completely destroyed. You are compassionate, just as a mother feels toward the baby she carries in her womb; that mood towards me never goes away. At the break of day the reaction of your mercy to me starts all over again. The firmness of my security in you is abundant.

✛

PSALMS 36:5 · PSALMS 103:8 · LAMENTATIONS 3:22, 23

You, Your, You Are

Webster's defines *you, your,* and *you* are as; the person being addressed; that which belongs to you; the present tense plural of the verb *to be*. To put it simpler the Bible is saying to us who God is; that is His disposition and character; what He possesses and the authority of His power. Also what He does or how He exhibits His character, power, and authority. We can see some of these qualities all throughout nature, but God's ultimate plan is to reveal these things in and towards man. It was man not nature that was created in His image. God is not nature; you won't find God in a plant or an animal. Man is His affection, His passion, and His ultimate intention.

Affection, Passion, Ultimate Intention

- His affection, devotion and love for man is superior to all His creation.
- He never changes who He is or reacts towards man outside of His love.
- God is kindhearted and concerned about us and our life.
- He gives us help when we need it.
- He is sympathetic and compassionate towards us in our pain and misery.
- We do not irritate or bother Him with our problems.
- He displays and we receive an overflow of what we do not deserve.
- God does not judge us according to what we deserve. He accepts and agrees to care for us.
- God is caring and gentle even when we are ignorant and immature.

● God's forgiveness is like the passing of each day; yesterday is over and your future is all that matters to Him.

What do you think you could ever do to earn these things? How could anyone be good enough and deserve such mercy in return? You cannot! That's just it. Love is God being God. It is Him desiring to become involved in all the affairs of man so He may lavish upon us all that He has and all that He is. God does not disappoint us; we fail to recognize Him because of false expectations and definitions of what REAL love is. All God requires from us is to believe Him; we cannot please Him or receive from Him without faith. The truth of God's love is not the same as the disappointments we have experienced in our past or the images society creates for us. It is the peace, serenity and rest we have inside us that neither circumstances nor people can ever take from us. It is imparted into us when we receive Christ into our lives by the confession and repentance of our past behavior, poor choices, and rebellion against God's Word. Do not suffer any longer; receive love and peace today.

✣

PRAYER: Ask for God to reveal His love to you.

MEMORIZE & MEDITATE: Psalms 103:8

FAITH ACTION: Repent and receive God's favor.

A God Perspective!

Destined

To Die, So We Could *Live*

CHAPTER TWENTY SEVEN

He DECLARED US NOT GUILTY

BECAUSE OF HIS GREAT *kindness*.

AND NOW WE KNOW THAT WE WILL

inherit ETERNAL LIFE.

Titus 3:7 (NLT)

My Confession

God selected you, Jesus, who never had felt the punishment of offending God's law by breaking it; and it was you who was changed into sin on my behalf that I might come into being what you were BEFORE, innocent and holy just as if I had never broken God's commands. You traded places with me before God, and it is in you and because of you that I am in this position. I believe in you and the work you did for me, and now I am not guilty of sin and declared blameless. No one can be declared sin free before you by performing ritualistic regulations in an attempt to satisfy your standards of living. Rather, it is crystal clear that holy people will live life by the assurance and moral conviction that they are sin and guilt free before you. Now that I am free and rendered innocent because of your favor towards me, I have become a "sharer", inheriting and possessing now in my life the anticipated pleasure of perpetual living.

✧

2 CORINTHIANS 5:21 · GENESIS 15:6

GALATIANS 3:11 · TITUS 3:7

Destined To Die So You Could Live

For every man death is inevitable. With all the buzz about discovering our destiny and purpose for life, what if you discovered yours was to grow up to suffer torture and death for another person? It seems that American Christianity is slowly becoming about "what I can get from God". Destiny and purpose for Christians is to simply surrender your life to God in order to obtain His life. I know that the destiny/purpose books teach us what God created us for, but most of what I hear and read is shaped around financial prosperity and the cultural nuances of America. I believe Jesus' life is the pattern for Christians. Our life is not all about us; rather what we can become for the benefit of others.

What Jesus did for us

1. He took upon Himself the punishment we deserved and became our substitute.

2. He became sin for us that we might become holy in God's sight. He transferred to us.

3. We are now accepted as a child of God. Recognition.

4. We are innocent and not guilty of breaking God's law. We have been pardoned and forgiven.

5. We do not need to perform religious ceremonies in order to receive God's mercy and pardon. We cannot earn God's favor.

6. We remain guilt free of our sin by trusting in Jesus. Faith.

7. The goodwill of God enables us to receive the supernatural, abundant life He promised us. Grace.

Romans 8:29 says, "*For those God foreknew he also predestined to be conformed to the likeness of his Son*". Our destiny and purpose is to become like Jesus. What if all throughout our life we looked to do things for others we would want them to do for us? Would that be your purpose for living? How about giving what we have so that someone else can receive blessing instead of keeping for our benefit. Could we acknowledge the accomplishments of others above ourselves or forgive people when they deliberately hurt us? Can we be transparent before God and others rather than do things with selfish motives? What about acting on what God sets before us rather than complaining because of what we do not have. Maybe we just extend and give to people the very thing they do not deserve from us. Friend, this is purpose and destiny in Christ. This is true Christianity: to lay down your life for the benefit and blessing of someone else. Jesus Christ gave and lived the example we should follow. Does your faith and Christianity look like this?

✥

PRAYER: Ask God to show you the needs of others.

MEMORIZE & MEDITATE: Galatians 3:11

FAITH ACTION: Respond to the needs of others.

Your faithfulness endures forever!

Faithful God

faith

CHAPTER TWENTY EIGHT

For a *brief* moment I abandoned you, but

with great COMPASSION I will take you back.

In a moment of anger I turned my *face* away

for a little while. But with EVERLASTING love

I *will* have compassion on you.

Isaiah 54:7-8 (NLT)

My Confession

For the smallest and measurable amount of time you have left me destitute. But for the rest of history you have shown your mercy and tender love to me. Your rage towards me was so very small, you covered your favor from me just momentarily; but kindness, favor and your good deeds towards me is perpetual — never ending. You, the eternal God, are the one who paid my ransom. You have said you are merciful to me, but greater yet you have displayed your love and affection towards me. You declared 7 times with your lips an oath to never show your fury near me or to ever forsake me at anytime under any circumstances. For a mountain may cease to exist, and a hill may decay, but your promise to me is that your kindness and favor will never be withdrawn from me. The covenant of safety, happiness, health and prosperity will never depart from me. Because you love me and show your compassion, you have given your word that this is true.

✠

ISAIAH 54:7-10

FAITHFUL GOD

Faithful, consistently loyal, trustworthy, and steady are adjectives used to describe God. They not only describe Him, they define Him. Yet if we were to examine our lives would these same words define who we are? Probably not — the consistent part anyway. Nevertheless, God does not change. One day as a young man very discouraged about my behavior towards God, I read these words, 2 Tim 2:13 *"if we are faithless, he will remain faithful, for he cannot disown himself."* "God you mean that my failures cannot keep you from always loving me?" Nope! "You mean that I really am a part of who you are?" Yes! It was one of the most powerful experiences in my Christian walk. Just see how Isaiah describes faithfulness.

His faithfullness

1. From .0001 (infinity of 0's) of a second compared to eternity is the percentage difference that God was merciful and loving to being angry with us and forsaking us.

2. .0001 (infinity of 0's) of the size of an atom compared to the size of endless galaxies is the percentage difference between God's anger toward us and His kindness and favor.

3. Like galaxies, God's faithfulness to us never ends.

4. The everlasting God paid a debt for us so we could always be a part of Him.

5. God declares in an oath that if He ever breaks His promise to us and shows

His wrath, that He Himself would become the recipient of that anger instead of us.

6. God says He will not give us what we deserve, but He exhibits love and cares for us in our daily life.

7. Mt. Everest will dissolve before God takes away His favor and kindness from us.

8. A legal document signed with God's own blood in the courtroom of heaven says that safety, happiness, health and prosperity will never depart from us.

9. God's Word is always displayed with His action.

What activates the manifestation and benefits of God's faithfulness? Our faith. A friend once told me that the only unpardonable sin is unbelief. Everything we do must be acted upon with our faith; if we ever fail to believe God He cannot help us. I fear in my own life that when I reach heaven and look back on what could have been, I may be disappointed because I failed to believe God's Word. I may have allowed circumstances to rule my life. Let's not have this regret. Let's discover God's truth and act on it; He is the Faithful One that can never, ever disown Himself.

✣

PRAYER: Thank God for His faithfulness toward you.
MEMORIZE & MEDITATE: Isaiah 54:10
FAITH ACTION: Receive God's promises and act on them.

I belong to You!

THE *Lord* OUR *Righteousness*

CHAPTER TWENTY NINE

So NOW THERE IS NO CONDEMNATION FOR THOSE

WHO BELONG TO *Christ Jesus*.

Romans 8:1 (NLT)

My Confession

By Jesus everyone who believes in the work of the cross is declared righteous, free from punishment under God's law. Obeying rituals and being religious can never make me holy in God's sight. I am no longer under a death sentence if I am in agreement with Jesus. I go forward in life in HIS strength, being aware at all times it is because of the right standing he has with God, which he in turn transferred to me, that I can now live without guilt. His name is and I will call him Jehovah, THE LORD MY RIGHTEOUSNESS.

✚

ACTS 13:39 · ROMANS 8:1 · PSALMS 71:16

JEREMIAH 23:6

THE LORD OUR RIGHTEOUSNESS

The single greatest lie of the devil is that if man does his best and lives a good life then he will go to heaven. The Jews in the Old Testament continually tried to please God with their attempts to follow the law. Almost every religion known to man requires its followers to perform religious acts, or their behavior to be a certain way to have eternal life. If this is what is required we are all doomed before a Holy God. What is good enough? How much good can one person do? If the best people sometimes fail, and THEY can still go to heaven on their own merit, then God's law and His standards are flawed and imperfect also. But in fact the Christian is provided a way of acceptance by God now and in heaven. Only his belief in the finished work of Christ and the acceptance of HIS righteousness will allow him entrance, NOT his own acts of righteousness. Romans 3:20 *"no one will be declared righteous in his sight by observing the law; rather, through the law we become conscious of sin."* This is what Christians are to do and believe.

- Come to Jesus Christ.
- Believe that He, a righteous man, died in our place.
- He transferred His righteousness to us.
- Jesus took upon Himself the judgment we deserved.
- Religious customs and ceremonies cannot make us holy.
- We are not condemned to eternal separation from God.
- Live life in God's power, not our own.
- We are accepted and approved by God.

- We no longer need to carry the guilt of our past actions.
- Jesus is our righteousness and holiness before God.

We can live a righteous and holy life before God. It does not mean we are perfect or will never sin again, but trusting in the atoning sacrifice of Christ covers not only your past and present sin but your future sin as well. That does not give us a license to sin because to do so would be to crucify Jesus all over again. No, we have a person, Jesus who represents us if we sin. I John 2:1-2 says *"if anyone sins, we have an Advocate with the Father, Jesus Christ the righteous. And He Himself is the propitiation for our sins, and not for ours only but also for the whole world"*. An advocate is a lawyer, and propitiation is a sacrifice of atonement. Our lawyer represents us before God the judge in heaven declaring His sacrifice paid the penalty for ALL our sins; therefore, we His client, are not guilty because we trust and believe in His sacrifice. God then does an amazing thing; not only does He declare us not guilty, but He turns and declares us righteous, just as righteous as Jesus. So your choice is to stand before God on your own or with Jesus, which will you choose?

✢

PRAYER: Thank God for HIS righteousness upon you.

MEMORIZE & MEDITATE: Acts 13:39

FAITH ACTION: Confess with your mouth you are legally just as righteous as Jesus.

For You will make a way!

Insight
FOR OUR
Daily Living

FRIENDSHIP WITH THE *Lord*

IS RESERVED FOR THOSE WHO FEAR HIM.

With THEM HE SHARES THE

SECRETS OF HIS COVENANT.

Psalms 25:14 (NLT)

My Confession

The LORD confides and speaks in confidence to those who show respect and admiration toward him; he makes the promises of his covenant treaty known to them. Since I belong to and now share with Christ Jesus, I know he has become the wisdom and insight for my daily living that has come to life and is in material form for me. That wisdom for living is the equality of character, innocence, and right standing I now have with God. It is my state of purity and holiness before God my Father, knowing that Jesus paid in full a ransom for the deliverance of my soul. For the LORD gives wisdom, and from his mouth comes all the knowledge and understanding I need to live the abundant life on earth that he purchased for me.

✛

PSALMS 25:14 · 1 CORINTHIANS 1:30 · PROVERBS 2:6

*I*NSIGHT FOR OUR *D*AILY *L*IVING

Every Christian I know wants to live a life of victory, purpose, and significance. We all want to represent our Lord and Master well here on the earth. We want to live a life that enables others to see a Living Jesus in and through our life. Yet we become frustrated sometimes because of our own personal failures, and that can discourage us from serving God the way we would like. We become anxious because we want to do more for God than we have character and gifting for. We can see the potential of a situation and cannot achieve it because of other commitments, time, or lack of money. Maybe this is not you, and I am only talking about myself. Whichever one is true, the Bible gives us insight for how to live today.

- Show reverence to God at all times in all situations.
- Listen for God to speak to your heart daily.
- Allow God to disclose secrets in His Word to you daily.
- Let God reveal His personal promises to you.
- Live like you are part of something greater than yourself.
- Understand that you are under the ownership of God.
- You have the ability to make good decisions today.
- God can inform you of what will happen before it actually does.
- Making timely choices is a by-product of relationship.
- Know you are holy before God because of the finished work of Christ.
- God can give us the right information we need at the right time.

- He wants us to pursue Him for understanding our situations.

- He provided and makes the way for us in this life to be and to do all He intended for us.

What is the secret to daily successful living in this confession? It is the ability and desire to secure a daily time alone with God. It is about having a consistent devotional lifestyle whereby you and God are in constant communication. Some people call it a quiet time, others call it the secret place; regardless of your terminology, you need time each day to commune with the Holy Spirit. Worship, prayer, Bible reading and study, and meditation are all disciplines of a devotional life. King David started everyday early in the morning seeking God. When and where is not as important as doing it. Get alone with God daily for undistracted time. The insight for successful, daily living is knowing Jesus, loving Jesus, and spending time to worship Him. You must set aside daily time with God; it is the greatest investment and the smartest decision you will make everyday.

✦

PRAYER: Thank God He has provided a way for success.

MEMORIZE & MEDITATE: I Corinthians 1:30

FAITH ACTION: Establish a time and place to meet with God daily.

Lean not on your own understanding!

Wisdom *Heaven* FROM Heaven

CHAPTER THIRTY ONE

But the *wisdom* that comes from HEAVEN

is FIRST of all pure. It is also peace loving, gentle

at all times and willing to *yield* to others.

It is *full* of MERCY and good deeds.

James 3: 17 (NLT)

My Confession

"The power to be aware of and bring forth into reality the secrets and mysteries of the realm and reign of happiness and power for living have been given to me. The wisdom that comes from heaven is first of all pure, clean and modest; then peace-loving by being considerate and gentle toward others, submissive and compliant, full of mercy, compassion with good and beneficial results, impartial, unprejudiced and sincere — not pretending to be something that is not real. So if I have wisdom it will show by my good and honest actions in life, by my consistent behavior of not just thinking about myself but laboring for the benefit of others first. To the man who pleases Him, God gives wisdom, knowledge and happiness, but to the one who does not do the accepted thing in their behavior for God's standard of living, He gives the task of gathering and storing up wealth to hand it over to the one who pleases him.

✠

MATTHEW 13:11 · JAMES 3:17 · JAMES 3:13

ECCLESIASTES 2:26

WISDOM FROM HEAVEN

We have all dreamed about being the recipient of a wish granted by God, a genie, or something with powers to grant such a request. What would you wish for; wealth, fame, love, or world peace? Well, Solomon was given the opportunity. God told him to ask for one thing, anything, and he would grant it. What did he ask for? Wisdom. Because he asked for that, God granted him wealth and fame. In fact the Bible declares Solomon was the richest and wisest man to ever live, all because of one thing, wisdom. Did you realize that we have access to the same source Solomon had? We can have wisdom from heaven for everyday life! How can we get it? How do we know we have it?

Wisdom for everyday life

1. It already is given to us in God's written Word.
2. We have ways to measure and gauge what wisdom is and what it is not.
3. Wisdom is not used only for our benefit.
4. Wisdom is revealed in righteous actions.
5. We must know how to please God.
6. God is the source for all wisdom.
7. We store up wealth for our future.

Proverbs 9:10 says, "*The fear of the LORD is the beginning of wisdom: and the knowledge of the holy one is understanding*". To respect, admire, and to be reverent toward God is the start of the ability to judge correctly and to follow the best

course of action for any circumstance. Wisdom manifests itself in the selection of proper ends with the proper means for their accomplishment. You can have knowledge yet lack wisdom. You can have the understanding needed to make right decision but not apply wisdom. Wisdom requires fearing God; that is an admiration of God's majesty, and to be afraid of his wrath. An example to fear the Lord is, "What are you like when no one is watching?" Do you have the sense of the omnipresence of God, that He is watching and remembering everything you do? Yet this is only the beginning of knowing who God is in His nature, attributes, and power is the tie to understanding. So it is safe to say that the pursuit of knowing and being in relationship with Christ is of greater value than knowledge on any given subject. We spend millions of dollars to obtain knowledge, but wisdom is what makes knowledge valuable. Make it your goal and purpose in life not to only obtain knowledge but to pursue wisdom through the fear and admonition of the Lord.

✦

PRAYER: Thank God for your ability to get wisdom.

MEMORIZE & MEDITATE: James 3:17

FAITH ACTION: Decide to pursue God for wisdom through your daily fear and reverence of Him.

ALL PRAISE TO THE GOD AND FATHER OF OUR LORD *Jesus* CHRIST. HE IS THE SOURCE OF EVERY MERCY AND THE GOD WHO COMFORTS US. HE *comforts* US IN ALL OUR TROUBLES SO THAT WE CAN COMFORT OTHERS. WHEN *others* ARE TROUBLED, WE WILL BE ABLE TO GIVE THEM THE SAME COMFORT GOD HAS *given* US. YOU CAN BE SURE THAT THE MORE WE SUFFER FOR CHRIST, THE MORE GOD WILL *shower* US WITH HIS COMFORT THROUGH CHRIST. SO WHEN WE ARE WEIGHED DOWN WITH TROUBLES, IT IS FOR YOUR BENEFIT AND *salvation!* FOR WHEN GOD COMFORTS US, IT IS SO THAT WE, IN TURN, CAN BE AN ENCOURAGEMENT TO YOU. THEN YOU CAN *patiently* ENDURE THE SAME THINGS WE SUFFER. WE ARE CONFIDENT THAT AS YOU SHARE IN SUFFERING, YOU WILL ALSO SHARE *God's* COMFORT. *2 Corinthians 1:3-7* NLT

Jesus, THANK YOU FOR EVERY PERSON WHO HAS READ THIS BOOK. MAY THEY BE TOUCHED BY YOUR *hand* IN THE SAME WAY YOU TOUCHED OUR FAMILY. LORD, OUR DESIRE IS TO HONOR *You* AND RETURN TO YOUR WONDERFUL PEOPLE THE BLESSING OF YOUR WONDERFUL WORD. *May* IT COMFORT, ENCOURAGE, CHALLENGE, BLESS, AND PROVOKE THEM TO A LIFESTYLE OF *worship.* MAY THEY DRAW CLOSER TO YOU, LORD, AS YOU REACH OUT TO THEM ON THESE WRITTEN PAGES. LET THEM EXPERIENCE THE LIVING *Christ* AS NEVER BEFORE. LET THEM CHANGE THE WORLD AROUND THEM FOR YOUR *glory.*

✝

Amen

Printed in the United States
45171LVS00002B/22-120

9 780977 648429